A Well That Keeps Flowing

A Well That Keeps Flowing

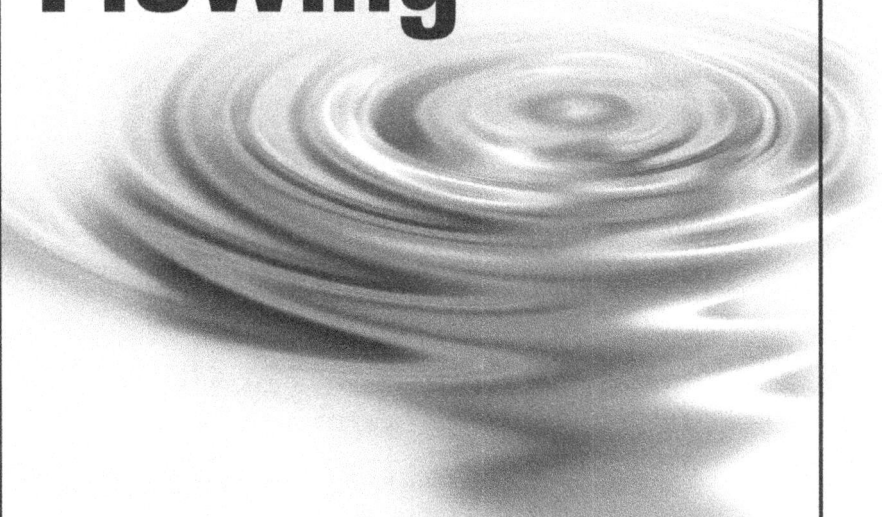

The Power of Co-Counseling

Fred Wallace, Ph D

Cover design: Millward and Millward Graphic Design
Stamford, Connecticut
Interior Design by the author
Logo - Co-Counseling Community of Scotland

Library of Congress Control Number: 2014921546
Be Your Greatness Press, New Haven, CT 06511

A Well that Keeps Flowing: The Power of Co-Counseling /
Fred Wallace
p. cm.
ISBN: 0986223107
ISBN 978-0-9862231-0-5

1. Wellness. 2. Emotions. 3. Feelings. 4. Self-help. 5. Co-
Counseling.

Author's note
The names used in the book are actual people except in one
case where the person's identity has been changed.

ISBN: 0986223107
Library of Congress Control Number: 2014921546
Be Your Greatness, New Haven, CT

To Chris,
the New Haven Co-Counseling Community,
and Co-Counselors around the world
who understand what it means to be human.

Acknowledgements

My warmest thanks goes to you, the readers, who share this book and the concept of Co-Counseling with friends and family. I trust this simple human process will reach all those who want to find peace within themselves and in their lives.

To the many friends who loved, cared, and stood by me as I wrote this book I extend my heart-felt gratitude. I would never had been finished it without your support. Cleveland Gardner believed from the beginning and gave me his huge Random House Dictionary along with a continuous stream of solid advice and wisdom. James Crook read an initial draft at a Co-Counseling conference in Hungary and encouraged me to keep writing. Cheryl Pytel, Barbara Woodis Ihloff, Rex McCann, and Phoebe Williams read the second draft and told me I could do better. Neik Sickenga, from the Netherlands, explored the book from the perspective of a European, pointing out American idioms that he didn't understand so I replaced them with clear meaningful English. Ágota Rusza from Hungary and Joke Stassen from the Netherlands inspired me to explore better ways to articulate my thoughts so they would have a more universal meaning. Louise Cox, David Vania, Minke Weggermans, Liz Bochain, and Andrew Feinstein reviewed the third draft and encouraged me to keep improving. Andrew took it upon himself to show me how to be a more powerful writer. Russell Schimmer after reading the third draft took it upon himself to sit with me week after week teaching me the elements of grammar I had missed growing up. Skip Short methodically examined every sentence in each draft, suggesting ways to improve the text. Peter Millward designed the cover and helped me in many little ways. Adam Bass, Holly Danowski, and Tim Fisher stood with me with their smiles and warm hearts. My friends at the Connecticut Men's Gathering cheered me on and encouraged me every time we met. The New Haven Co-Counseling community kept me on course in my determination to produce a beautiful book. My Co-Counseling companions and friends in Europe, New Zealand, San Francisco, New England and across the United States inspired me with their belief in Co-Counseling as a way to move their lives and be wonderfully human. And lastly, and firstly in my heart, I thank Chris Sanders, my partner, who gave me the biggest thesaurus money could buy, listened and stood with me in my doubts and joys, unwavering in her belief in me and the importance of this book.

Together
We work hard
Creating lives we can love
Staying conscious
We grow

Contents

A WELL THAT KEEPS FLOWING

Preface

This book is my personal exploration and examination of Co-Counseling as practiced within the guidelines of Co-Counseling International (CCI). The book describes my thoughts and vision based on maintaining a personal practice for thirty years and teaching Co-Counseling to hundreds of people. My hope is that the book will stimulate interest in Co-Counseling by those unfamiliar with it and inspire further inquiry into it by current practitioners.

CCI Co-Counseling is the largest self-counseling modality in the world. It is a global federation of independent self-help communities whose members are trained in the culture and practice of Co-Counseling. At its foundation is an insistence on peer relationships and self-responsibility. Each community is autonomous, developing its own decision-making procedures, establishing its own designs for training new members, and setting guidelines for becoming a trainer, or teacher. International, national, and local gatherings occur throughout the year. During these CCI events cocounselors share information about, inquire into, and practice the art of Co-Counseling. CCI continues to evolve to meet the needs and desires of individual members and communities.

CCI grew out of Re-Evaluation Counseling (RC), which was developed by Harvey Jackins in Seattle, Washington, in the 1950s and 1960s. It spread across the United States and Western Europe. However, as it grew it became "theoretically rigid and internally authoritarian,"[1] resulting in many people becoming disenchanted with RC. In 1973 John Heron, the University of Surrey in England, and Tom and Dency Sargent, Change Agents, Inc., Connecticut, left RC and formed CCI.

Any epigraph found under a chapter title that does not have a direct reference is from one of my self-published books of poetry.

Lastly, starting in chapter 22, I have alternated female and male pronouns to maintain gender neutrality.

THE POWER OF CO-COUNSELING

In this book:

- The term **Co-Counseling** refers to the modality or concept itself.

- The terms **to cocounsel** and **cocounseling** refer to the act whereby the concept becomes an actual practice in what is called a **session**.

- The term **cocounselor (s)** refers either to anyone who has successfully completed the Fundamentals training or to anyone in the act of cocounseling.

- The term **co-counselor** refers to the role of the listener in the act of cocounseling.

- The term **self-counselor** refers to the role of the speaker in the act of cocounseling.

For example: *In January 2015,* **cocounselors** *gathered for an international* **Co-Counseling** *workshop in New Zealand where they* **cocounseled**, *splitting their time equally between the roles of* **co-counselor** *and* **self-counselor** *while working in* **sessions**

The art and practice of living well in the 21st
Century

Introduction

Co-Counseling
Self-Education for the Heart

We live in the shadow of our own potential, and most
people know this on a conscious or unconscious level. All
of us believe somewhere deep inside that there is more
to us than we manifest in the world of our daily lives. Self-
education begins with a genuine desire to know ourselves
and to realize our potential. For some of us the desire
starts when our life falls apart or loses some of its excitement and satisfaction. For others the desire has always
been there. Behind the desire to learn about ourselves is
the belief there is something more in us. This belief leads
directly to an examination of our lives. But where do we
go to pursue a meaningful exploration of the self?

There are many wonderful books by brilliant and
thoughtful people about everything from history to bi-
ology, from meditation to yoga. There are many, many

insightful self-help books, as well as religious, psychological, and spiritual texts, but who actually teaches us? There are stimulating lectures and sermons filled with truths about life and living, but all these wise teachers can only present their ideas. It is we who have to grab the ideas and take them into our lives. No one else can do it for us. The truth is you and I are the experts on our own lives. We can hear the words of others, but we have to apply what we hear to ourselves. We ask ourselves: *Does that apply to me?* or *Is that true?* And how do we know if it is true or that it applies to us? We measure (or test) the idea against our own experience. Our experience provides us with the empirical data we need to make judgments, not only about ourselves, but about the entire world. Our own life experience is the best resource for understanding ourselves. So where do we go to learn from our own unique life experience?

If I am studying a subject such as physics or history, I would go to a library or the internet, where all the information about the subject can be found. In the same way, if the subject of my study is myself, I need to take the time to go where all the information about me is stored. I don't have to go to a library to find the information—I am the library! So in order to learn about myself, all I have to do is take the time to enter my own library, sit in one of those sections marked "quiet please," and start digging into the wealth information inside me.

THE POWER OF CO-COUNSELING

This is where the genius of Co-Counseling shines. As the basis of true self-education, Co-Counseling invites us to begin our exploration of ourselves by accepting ourselves as human. We take the time and space to walk through the gateway of our own humanity, leaving behind the complexity and issues attached to our external identity. Here we can experience the wonder of being human and begin our self-education from a place of heart-felt gratitude for simply being alive. We can then focus on the issues of everyday life, explore our past, and contemplate our future. And we do this while another person is witnessing us with a compassionate heart. Then we switch places with the person and take the time to witness them as they explore their world from the centered place of their humanness. Co-Counseling is built on the belief that we share a common humanity that we can access in the loving presence of another human being.

Part I

My Journey into Co-Counseling

Chapter 1

The Night

Today has been perfect

It was hard
I struggled
I smiled

Today has been perfect

One night in the fall of 1982 a sharp pain suddenly ripped through my belly. I was 40 years old and in good health. The pain overpowered me, and I collapsed onto the floor clutching my knees. My gut seemed to be exploding. White-hot spasms of pain filled every corner of my body. My head hit the floor, and I lay still, consumed by the pain. Suddenly I pushed myself onto my knees and held onto the bed. My body started rocking and swaying. I had no control over it as I gyrated from side to side. Then a primordial loud, deep bellowing poured out of me. I had not made the sound. It simply escaped from the depths of my being. I was overwhelmed with pain, confusion, and fear.

Five weeks earlier my second wife and her son had moved out of our new home. We decided to separate in peace before ending up resenting or hating each other. We filed for a no-fault divorce, and she left the house only after the divorce was granted. Once again I was a totally responsible for raising my beautiful young daughter, whom I loved deeply despite feeling inept as a single parent. Doubts about my ability to be a good father and make a decent living plagued me. I felt isolated as a single man raising a daughter and I am sure my daughter felt a similar isolation. I had no one to talk with and relied totally on Dr. Spock's baby book as my guide to parenting. I was beginning to hate being alone.

Now, on the floor next to my bed, erratically swaying back and forth in agony while a hideous howl roared out of my mouth, I was aware of nothing except my tormented being. I had no name beside the bed. I knew I was me, but it didn't make any difference because no reality existed other than the pain and the woeful noise. I could not move. I began wondering if this is how I was going to die.

Tears began rolling down my face as the awful sound kept thundered out of my body. The pain would subside and then roar back accompanied by the deep, hollow wailing.

THE NIGHT

I felt like a wounded animal in agony, howling into an empty night. The more the pain screamed within me, the more the tears flowed and the more the mournful bellowing roared.

After what seemed like forever, the intensity of the pain diminished, and the howling became a long series of anguished moans. Spaces grew between the waves of pain and silence between the moans. In these gaps my brain started functioning again. This was my bedroom. I was on the floor next to my bed, exhausted and confused with no idea of what precipitated the attack. I simply lay there panting, feeling the remnants of the pain, feeling the wetness of the tears on my face, and hearing the echoes of the animal sound lingering in my ears.

I suddenly thought of my daughter sleeping in her bedroom on the far side of the apartment. I prayed she had not been woken by the mournful bellowing. I needed to check on her. Using the bed for support I pulled myself onto my feet. As I began walking, I stumbled and grabbed the dresser to keep from falling. My body started shaking again and kept shaking. Slowly I relaxed and the shaking subsided. I forced myself to stand without support and after maybe the third try was able to start walking. Holding onto anything that could support me, I made it out of the bedroom, through the living room and the kitchen, to my daughter's bedroom, where I quietly opened the door and peaked in. She was sound asleep and did not stir as the kitchen light illuminated her room. I closed the door, got a glass of water, and collapsed onto the couch in the living room.

At first all I could do was sip the water and stare blankly into space as the room pulsated around me. I began paying attention to my breath, and ever so slowly the room settled down and came into clear focus. But as it did the pain started coming back. This time, however, it didn't take root in me because I could see its source. I was feeling the pain of my second marriage ending in failure. We no longer wanted the same things. Our love had dissolved into a litany of disappointments and disagreements. We actually liked each other, but could not be life partners. We had had five good years, and now it was ending. Logically this made sense to me. We had congratulated ourselves on how peaceably our relationship ended. She and her son left with hugs, goodbyes, and tears. I looked forward to being alone again with my daughter, who had been with me since she was three.

Everything went well for a time, but I started feeling empty. I started missing my wife. Suddenly the issues we had didn't seem important. My heart started to long for her smile and physical touch. The unknown world in front of me looked bleak, making my world with her seem secure and good. Having her in my life, even with all the problems, started to seem preferable to my life without her.

It was easy to blame my first wife for the end of that marriage. One afternoon, during what seemed like the hundredth heated argument, she threw a glass at me. I was sitting on the couch and caught the glass as it bounced off a cushion next to me. Filled with anger, I got up and walked toward her with the intent of smashing the glass into her face. But luckily something happened inside me in the ten steps between couch and where she stood. When I got in front of her, I simply handed her the glass, told her I was leaving, and walked out the door. I don't know what happened in the short time between catching the glass and giving it back to her, but I am eternally grateful it did. I left angry, self-righteous, and empowered. I was free, alive, and in motion. I put all the blame on her, denying my part in the failed marriage. Feeling good about myself for having left the relationship, I simply went on with my life.

Now, despite wanting my second marriage to end, I had no sense of empowerment, righteousness, or movement. I felt lonely. Even worse, a rumbling sense of personal failure began to haunt me. I was alone and unsupported. Every decision seemed difficult, and life began wearing me down. Without my partner the responsibilities of parenthood seemed endless. I no longer saw myself as an optimist. For the first time in my life I began looking at myself. What I saw scared me.

What was my part in this failed marriage? What was wrong with me that both my marriages failed? My answers were not flattering. I was still very much a boy who needed to grow up. My responsibility for my daughter seemed overwhelming. There was no one to help. Alone in my responsibility I simply needed to keep moving forward. Doubts flooded my mind, leaving me in a place barren of dreams.

Hunched over on the living room couch, I began understanding the sources of the burning pain that had overwhelmed me. The agony was based on my sense of personal failure for having lost the person I loved. The fear in my belly had been increasing for days along with my growing sense of being alone. The pain and anguish burst forth and overpowered me this night, reducing me to a deeply wounded, scared creature. I knew I would always remember this night. Being alone now terrified me.

I didn't understand the actual dynamics of the intense pain that just burned through me or the bellowing that filled my ears and heart, and I didn't care. I sat on the couch rocking back and forth, holding my head, and began to cry. I got up and closed the door to the kitchen to make sure my daughter didn't hear me and cried, talked to myself, and cried some more. I was alone and scared, feeling confused and ashamed about what just happened. I didn't want anyone to see me like this. This night would have to remain a secret.

And then I started thinking of my daughter. What was really going on for her? How was she handling this change? I was responsible for raising her, yet I doubted my ability to be a good parent. I couldn't get by on my own. Crawling into bed that night, I knew I needed help.

Chapter 2

Taking the First Step

The movement of descent and discovery begins at the moment you consciously become dissatisfied with life. Contrary to most professional opinion, this gnawing dissatisfaction with life is not a sign of "mental illness," nor an indication of poor social adjustment, not a character disorder. For concealed within this basic unhappiness with life and existence is the embryo of a growing intelligence, a special intelligence usually buried under the immense weight of social shams. A person who is beginning to sense the suffering of life is, at the same time, beginning to *awaken* to deeper realities, truer realities. For suffering smashes to pieces the complacency of our normal fictions about reality, and forces us to become alive in a special sense – to see carefully, to feel deeply, to touch ourselves and our worlds in ways we have heretofore avoided. It has been said, and truly I think, that suffering is the first grace. In a special sense, suffering is almost a time of rejoicing, for it marks the birth of creative insight.

—Ken Wilber, *No Boundaries*

In the days following that night, I found a therapist and went to see him. He asked me questions about my life, and I obediently answered. I tried to tell him about the pain in my belly, which I still felt, but he seemed more interested in doing some kind of profile on me. I returned to him twice more, but during the third time when he still seemed uninterested in what was happening to me in the present, I left, never to return.

I was overwhelmed with doubts about who I was and my ability to maintain my life as a full-time single parent and breadwinner. My distress led to confrontations with my teenage daughter, who sensed my weakness and challenged me at every turn. In retrospect I see that she was fighting for her own survival and seeking a level of security I could not provide. I was able to keep earning a living, although I expected my job could end at any time and my world would fall apart. I hated going to bed because I would lay awake worrying. I didn't like my life, but I didn't have a clue how to change it.

My Journey Into Co-counseling

I needed to talk to someone. I needed to share my doubts and pain and have someone tell me I was ok. I found another therapist, who evidenced interest in my inner life. Soon, however, he started interrupting me with questions about my relationships with my mother and my first wife. All I cared about was making it through the next day. When I said so, he insisted the information he wanted was necessary to understand the present. Now I understand he was probably right; at the time, however, his approach made no sense. I lasted for nine sessions and did not return.

Sometime thereafter, I heard of a woman who was referred to as a "holistic" counselor. I was told she was genuinely different from most therapists, and at the time that is all I needed to hear. I called, made an appointment, and arrived at the address I had been given. A beautiful woman with long brown hair opened the door. She introduced herself as Deborah, invited me in, and asked me to leave my shoes at the door. When we started the session, she asked me why I came. I just started talking about my night of pain and bellowing, doubts about myself, issues with my daughter, and my frustration with the two therapists. The session went by quickly, and as it ended she commented in a clear, non-judgmental voice that I had a lot of anguish built up inside me and that simply letting it out was what I needed. She said the real work of healing happened between sessions. She wanted me to decide what I thought were the most important things that had happened during the session and be ready to explore them in our next meeting.

Driving home, I experienced a sense of lightness. I had talked about what was going on, and Deborah listened. She asked a few questions, which helped me become aware of things I might have otherwise missed. She never really seemed to judge anything I said. A couple of times she asked me if I had heard what *I* had said. She accepted my "yes" to her questions without saying anything, except once, when she dramatically asked, "Did you *really hear* what you said?" I had stated, "I did not know what I was doing." With her encouragement I repeated it several times and then started crying. She simply handed me a tissue. When I stopped crying, she handed me another tissue and asked me how I felt. I confessed I was scared and didn't know what to do.

By the time I got home, I knew the two most important things that happened in the session were my acknowledging that I was scared and that I didn't know what I was doing. What relief I felt having admitted to my fear and confusion in front of another person. Deborah had simply listened to me with a gentle intensity. I am not sure I have ever had anyone listen to me like that before. I was smiling broadly when I entered my apartment. I felt better.

11

The session dominated my thinking during the next week. I reaffirmed that admitting I was scared and didn't know what I was doing were the most important things that happened. I was finally saying out loud what I had been thinking for months. I wanted to be prepared to answer the question when she asked it. I was determined to impress her.

At the beginning of the second session, when Deborah asked what I found important in the first session, I told her and plunged into an explanation. Deborah watched me, and when I finished, she asked if I had given any thought to my crying. I admitted I had. "And why didn't you think that was important?" she asked. I told her that every time I thought about admitting I was scared and didn't know what to do, I felt like crying again. I told her I felt weak and sad in those moments. "So you thought about the fact you cried, and you didn't think it was important?" She sounded skeptical. I knew I felt ashamed for having cried. Each time I thought about it, I felt tears building up behind my eyes. I was a man, and men weren't supposed to cry, or at least that was the story I told myself. I didn't want to cry. I wanted to be strong, especially in front of a beautiful woman. "So why didn't you mentioned it?" she asked. I remained silent even though I knew why. I was embarrassed because I couldn't keep control of my emotions. I felt it made me seem weak and out of control. After a bit she repeated her question, and when I finally started answering, I began crying. Again

12

I felt weak and out of control, which made me cry even more. When I stopped she asked me what I was feeling, and I honestly told her. I was embarrassed and felt weak. She smiled, looking at me with her clear brown eyes, and said something to the effect that it was good I was finally willing to speak my truth. I looked at her and began crying again.

At the end of our hour I agreed to come back for ten more sessions. She walked me to the front door. When I turned to open the door, she tapped me on the shoulder and told me that hugging was part of our session work. She stepped forward and hugged me. I was intensely uncomfortable with her hugging me. My brain was racing with questions about why this beautiful woman hugging was me. The hug, rather than what had happened during the session, dominated my thoughts for the week before we met again.

At the beginning of the third meeting, Deborah started out commenting on my extreme nervousness when she hugged me. She asked me to talk about it. Summoning up every bit of my courage, I told her that for me hugs with women were strongly sexual and that *the hug* dominated my thoughts during the week. She probed and challenged me about why I would think it was sexually based. I told her for me hugs between a man and a woman was always sexual. I had never shared a hug that wasn't. She explained that by hugging me she was extending friendship and respect.

Through the hug she was telling me she trusted me. She had me talk about my history of hugging, which I did. From that point on we hugged at the beginning and end of each session. She was my counselor and, therefore, she was safe (non-sexual). I enjoyed the hugs and slowly began feeling genuine connected with her through the hugs. I felt our relationship was extraordinary.

My life had fallen apart, but now I was beginning to pick up the pieces and was discovering new pieces along the way. I had found help.

Chapter 3

Taking the Next Step

I can tell you what I do
I can tell you what I believe
I can tell you what I like and want
I can tell you of my dreams
And
Who am I?

I am the third son of a middle-class family with four healthy children and two parents. My father worked hard six days a week. His responsibility was to earn the money to support the family. My mother stayed home and raised the family, cooked the meals, and kept the house neat and clean. I was bright, inquisitive, and quiet, with a tendency to isolate myself. My inquisitiveness and red-haired anger sometimes got me in trouble, but on the whole I seemed to get along well in the world. I had no particular dreams but was determined to be successful, whatever that meant.

My Journey Into Co-counseling

I remembered the obvious facts and events of my child-hood but had never explored or examined my internal life as a child or as an adult. I didn't see myself as much different from most middle-class white kids growing up in America in the late 1940s and 1950s. What I knew was, if I worked hard, success would eventually come my way.

I was who I was. I could change what I did and how I did it when I needed to accomplish some task or get what I wanted within my known world. I lived without thinking about who I was. I lived in the world of an immortal youth who had never known death, devastating disappointment, or earth-shattering trauma. I had experienced occasional disappointment and failure, but nothing had destroyed my faith in myself until the night of the bellowing.

I had never given much thought to who I was. I did what was in front of me. That is what I was taught—you just go through life doing what you have to do. Now in my fortieth year, talking about my life to a holistic counselor, I was finding out about me.

During the sessions with Deborah, it dawned on me how naive I was about myself. She didn't let me blame anyone for my life. "What's your part?" she asked over and over when I whined or complained about something. She kept asking simple questions about me and how I lived my life.

16

Many times I had no idea what to say in response to her questions, and then she would guide me to where I could find an answer. She repeatedly pointed out that I was the only one responsible for my decisions. I was becoming aware *I* was living my life. I was beginning to understand things I had never thought about: Who was I? How did I get here? How did my history impact who I was?

Only later did I recognize that the process of learning about me was laying the groundwork for my life journey. My life had to fall apart before I could consciously re-create it. I was learning that who I am, is a matter of choice, not simply a matter of established, unchanging facts acquired in childhood. I could change, but part of me had to die in order for that change to happen.

Near the end of the ten sessions, Deborah strongly recommended I join a men's group that was just forming. In celebration of being forty, I thought, *why not?* At the first meeting I discovered most of the men already knew each other. I immediately felt the familiar feeling of being an outsider. These men were vibrant, loud, and not afraid to speak about their lives in detailed ways I had never heard anyone talk. During the first several meetings I said very little, more an observer than a participant. I would drive to each meeting fearful the men would challenge me to share like they shared and drove home relieved that they hadn't. One night I almost turned around on my way to a

17

meeting but kept going because I had promised Deborah I would attend ten sessions.

The openness of the men truly surprised me. Deborah was the first and only person I had even spoken to with such honesty. The men freely shared details about their lives that I would never reveal. Listening, I learned they were dealing with difficult personal issues on a daily basis. They were being truthful about their struggles, while I sat feeling little and scared. I could not speak about my life the way they were speaking about theirs. They not only talked about being angry, sad, and scared, they physically engaged these emotions by shaking out fear, pounding out anger, and shedding tears of sadness. I had never been around such displays of emotion and was fascinated and terrified. I felt a lot of the same emotions but kept them tightly contained inside.

As time passed I became more comfortable with what transpired in the meetings. I was attracted to the liveliness of the group yet terrified that they expected me to share as honestly as they did. The only thing I could honestly say about myself was that I was confused. My life had been ripped open, and I was scrambling to put it back together. Although I said very little, the men seemed to accept me as one of them. At the end of the ten sessions, I knew I had to continue.

One of the men, Michael, found out I liked canoeing. He was an avid canoeist and invited me to join him and a couple of the other men for day-trips down the rivers of Connecticut. On these outings I talked about my thoughts concerning the group and began sharing buried aspects of my life more openly. It was easier for me to share with just one or two men rather than with the whole group. I realized I was trusting them in ways I had never trusted men. Before meeting with them, I had preferred the company of women because I could talk with them about my issues, especially about raising my daughter. The few men I hung out with never talked about personal matters. Now I was with a group of men who were not afraid to talk about what was really going on in their lives, and I was becoming their friend. I trusted them and began to speak truthfully about my life, and they listened. My life was changing.

Chapter 4

Finding Co-Counseling

I hugged a tree
Firmly holding it in my arms
Feeling its immense power and energy.
I was at peace.

Only the spirits of the forest
Witnessed my hug.
I was safe.

Men in the group began suggesting I take a Co-Counseling
Fundamentals training. Michael, in particular, kept telling me how much I would get from the training. Most
of these men were cocounselors and spoke in glowing
terms about the training. They explained that many of
the things we did in the men's group came directly from
Co-Counseling. They said it would give me a different understanding of my life as well as help me gain access to
my emotions. They said they learned to speak about and
physically engage their emotions in the Co-Counseling

training. After several months of quietly suggesting I take the training, they, with Michael in the lead, began harassing me about getting off my ass so I could start doing some *real work* in the group. For months the rebel in me kept them at bay, but I finally said yes.

I signed up for a Co-Counseling Fundamentals training. The trainer was a woman named Barbara, the wife of one of the men in the group and a good friend of Deborah. I went to the first class, and in some ways it was like my men's group. Barbara was warm and inviting. We met in her living room and sat on the floor. I don't remember anyone from the course except Diane, who worked where I used to work. I was happy to see her but felt a little strange seeing her outside the work context. The class was mostly women, and Barbara enjoyed a strong relationship with many of them. I was not sure why, but I did not feel as safe in the class as I did in the men's group.

At the end of our first meeting, Barbara started hugging everyone and people started hugging each other, including me. I let myself be hugged without really hugging back and then somehow exited the house. I was especially uncomfortable hugging Diane, even though she seemed glad to hug me.

I grew up in a home where hugging, as well as all forms of affectionate touch, stopped at about the age of puberty.

My Journey Into Co-counseling

The only physical contact I really remember was being spanked by my father or slapped by my mother and fighting with my brothers. I did not hug my mother or father, and they did not hug me. Hugging between men and women was from novels, movies, and magazines and definitely had a strong sexual component. Except for Deborah, hugging women for me was always part of a sexual dance.

I learned to hug men in my men's group. At first I merely accepted hugs from these men, but then I relaxed and began giving hugs as well as receiving them. The hugs conveyed the affection and trust we held for each other. Sometimes we shared hugs in the spirit of celebration. This act of supportive connection was an ordinary part of our meetings. Hugging men was relatively easy for me to adjust to because it was clearly non sexual for me and, therefore, had no implications beyond the hug itself.

In the second meeting of the Co-Counseling training, Barbara explained that physical touch in the forms of handholding and hugging was part of the Co-Counseling culture. She talked about how all touch was for the purpose of grounding and nurturing and said in her clear, strong voice that this was counter-cultural. In America we had sexualized touch, therefore, people avoided this simple act of affection and respect. She also talked about how we are totally responsible for ourselves. If we didn't want to hold hands or hug a person, we were to simply say *no* or *no thank you*. There was no need to give an explanation. In Co-Counseling you have the full power of your *no* and your *yes*. Having been a *yes* person my whole life, part of my new work was learning to say *no*.

We then did an exercise in which we wandered around the room and asked people for a hug. We all had the right to ask the question and all had the right to say *yes* or *no* when the question was asked of us. I acted through the exercise doing what I was supposed to do. I didn't like asking for a hug from people I barely knew, and I didn't want to say *no* because I might offend the person asking me for the hug. I got through the exercise and, in the sharing circle that followed, spoke honestly about my dilemma. No advice was given. It was my issue, and I had to deal with it.

In the men's group I talked about the Co-Counseling training and my problem with hugging women and my *yes-no* struggle. They all agreed that learning to say *no* was critical to my being truly self-responsible. Someone in the group said that my *yes* was only as meaningful as my *no* was meaningful. That kicked off a discussion that lasted the whole evening. It turned out that many of the men had as difficult a time saying *no* as I did. Saying *no* as children was not accepted, and so many of the men,

MY JOURNEY INTO CO-COUNSELING

like me, developed a pattern of never saying *no* or feeling
guilty when they did say *no*. I was shocked that so many
of these men, who I saw as strong and powerful, had this
same issue. After that I felt more of an equal in the men's
group.

At the end of the meeting several of the men assured me
that the sexual content of the hugs in the Co-Counseling
training would quickly fade as I got to know the women
as people. They were right. By the time the class ended I
was putting energy into the hugs, fully embracing all the
people in the class—except Diane. (Although I hugged
her, the hugs felt perfunctory rather than whole-heart-
ed.) I was learning that these hugs were as nurturing and
grounding as were those in the men's group. I began to
fully appreciate the warmth and spirit of a good hug.

24

Chapter 5

Co-Counseling Basics

An honest step forward
Requires little energy
Truth gives wings to the feet

The Co-Counseling training was clear and simple. The class was experiential, meaning we were taught skills and techniques, practiced them, and applied them in short exercises. Every time we practiced a technique or a skill, we had the chance to relate our experience in what is called a *sharing circle*. In these circles each person got the opportunity to talk about the exercise and ask questions. Each of us always had the right to *pass*, meaning we didn't have to say anything if we didn't want to. I liked what I was learning, especially some of the strength building exercises, which I immediately took into my daily life.

At the heart of the Co-Counseling process are two people paired together in what is called a *session*. Within a session there are two distinct roles: the self-counselor and the co-counselor. In the role of the self-counselor a person actively engages, examines, plans, and celebrates her life. The person is totally in charge of what she does and how she does it. At first this caused me real problems because I didn't know how to examine my life. The two therapists I encountered totally directed and controlled my time with them. With Deborah I could talk more freely about my life, but she suggested things for me to work on, helped me stay focused, and guided me toward finding answers. In the men's group, advice was freely given. In Co-Counseling no one directed me.

As the training went on we were taught skills and techniques to guide and deepen our work in the role of the self-counselor. I learned how to sort through issues and stay focused on one thing at a time. I learned I could enter into the mysteries of my life and emerge with truths I had not been aware of. I was making connections between how I was raised and how I lived as an adult. I was discovering my emotions could be my friends. We practiced a technique called *free association,* and through it I discovered an innate intelligence inside me I had never been conscious of but had used many times. This intelligence, which resides in all of us, became my conscious companion helping me guide my work.

After four or five weeks I was truly becoming my own self-counselor. I could actively choose what I was working on and how I was working on it while not being afraid of what I found. Lastly we were taught several ways to bring the realizations and knowledge we gained as the self-counselor directly into our lives. "What are you taking from your work?" was a question continually asked when we did sharing circles.

The role of the co-counselor seemed much easier to me. All I had to do was sit quietly and provide the self-counselor with what is called *caring-aware-attention*. In this role I was not supposed to judge, evaluate, or attempt to fix the person working on his life. "Just to be there," Barbara said, "is an amazingly powerful part of the Co-Counseling session." It was natural for me to just sit there without saying anything because I learned early in life to keep my mouth shut. Too often I had opened my mouth and immediately got in trouble. Although I really liked listening without any responsibility for the person sitting across from me, I found keeping my brain from making judgments much harder. Just because I had learned to keep my mouth shut didn't mean I wasn't judging what people said all the time. During some of my first times in the co-counselor role, I wanted to scream at the person across from me because I thought I could see clearly what he was unable to see. I had to be silent. After a while my brain became quiet and I could sit without wanting to direct the other person's work.

My Journey Into Co-counseling

As the co-counselor I was to look continuously at the person's eyes. No matter where he looked or if he had his eyes closed, I was to maintain contact with his eyes, not staring but looking softly at him. The power of this I discovered while in the role of the self-counselor. Sometimes I worked with my eyes closed because I could concentrate more easily on what was happening inside me. Whenever I opened my eyes, the person in the co-counselor role would be looking directly at me. It was through his eyes that I felt the connection with him. Having his eyes focused on me seemed to bring me back into myself if I had lost my focus in the work I was doing. Somehow, having him looking at me told me he was hearing what I was saying and fully accepting it. So through the role of the self-counselor I learned how important it was to maintain *eye contact* in the role of the co-counselor. In fact eye contact was the essential manifestation of *caring-aware-attention*.

In sharing circles I learned many people were having a hard time in this role. They could not keep their brains silent. They were sitting quietly in front of self-counselors maintaining *eye contact*, yet their brains were in over drive, evaluating, judging, and thinking up solutions to problems they were hearing. Some completely stopped giving attention to the other person because they were totally involved in battling the urge to evaluate and judge. I think I was the only one in the class who found it more difficult to work on my life than to stay focused on giving *caring-aware-attention,* a tribute to how deeply I learned to keep my mouth shut as a child.

Co-Counseling is a two-way process. The session consists of the participants having equal time as self-counselor and co-counselor. Half way through a session the two people switch roles. The person who was in the role of the self-counselor becomes the co-counselor, while the person who was the co-counselor becomes the self-counselor. Barbara repeatedly spoke about us all being peers in our humanity. We are all born of mothers, destined to die, and caught in the maelstrom of living in a world of relationships, jobs, and dreams. Therefore, I share a basic understanding of what it means to be human with all other humans regardless of age, race, ethnicity, gender, and economic circumstances. And so I can be the co-counselor for you and you can be the co-counselor for me. A real sense of human equality existed in the training; and the more we worked together the more we seemed similar than different.

Some concepts and ideas were deeply challenging; among these was the notion that I was completely responsible for my thoughts, feelings, and behavior. In the language of Co-Counseling I am 100% in charge of my life. Barbara stated that we cannot blame anyone for what we do, think, or feel. I found this hard to accept. In my work with Deborah the idea of being self-responsible was emphasized, but in Co-Counseling it became an essential part of how we live our lives. Barbara said no matter what happens in our lives, it is always our choice how we react and act. I didn't want to hear this because I always blamed others when things went wrong. I always saw myself as the innocent victim. Now I had to examine my part in creating my own life. I could no longer simply be the victim.

Chapter 6

An Issue of Trust

So during this daynight
The choices you make are all yours
There is no one to blame

I liked working with Barbara and most of the people in the training. When I was paired with Diane, my former co-worker, however, I found myself guarded and superficial. I began to wish she wasn't in the training. My previous workplace was rife with gossip; and Diane, who was in management, seemed to me to be in the epicenter of the whispering. I did not trust her.

From the beginning of the training, Barbara was emphatic about the importance of confidentiality. She repeatedly stated that everything said in a session or in a sharing circle was absolutely confidential. "What is said in a session stays in the session," was the phrase she used. Confidentiality meant that a person could do her work as the self-counselor without fear of having anything

31

she said or did referenced or talked about. Maintaining confidentiality was essential in Co-Counseling.*

Despite what Barbara said, I could not let myself believe Diane would not talk about me outside of class. I had seen and heard her gossip, and I did not want to be the subject of her small talk. I did not believe she would follow the rules. Simply put, I did not feel safe around her and did not trust her to hold confidentiality.

So as much as I enjoyed learning the skills and techniques taught, my lack of trust gnawed on me. I was discovering things about myself I wanted to share as part of the group but did not feel free to reveal. My fear of Diane's gossiping kept me from being fully engaged in my work. Worse, I blamed her for my not doing my work, and this became a source of a real personal dilemma. I tried to accept the Co-Counseling belief that I was completely responsible for my thoughts, feelings, and behavior while, at the same time, I was blaming her for my reticence to share openly. I talked about this in my men's group, and a number of men encouraged me to speak up, but I remained silent.

---

* In her poem *Jury Service* the Scottish poet Margaret Christie, who is a cocounselor, writes:

> I can't tell you what went on between the jurors.
> I'm sworn to silence for ever and ever, an extreme
> Of secrecy matched, perhaps, by the confidentiality rule
> In Co-Counselling...[2]

An Issue Of Trust

I didn't have the courage to say anything. So what was I even doing in the class? I felt ashamed. I was stuck being a victim of my own inability to act.

When I was paired with Diane, I talked about my job and was amazed at the insights I got about my work and the people I worked with every day. These sessions were profitable even though I carefully avoided talking about anything personal. In the sharing circles I simply did not share any content I thought was too personal.

I hungered to be truthful, but my fear that Diane would talk about me kept me from being open and honest. Her presence was simply ruining the training for me. I kept attending the classes but kept my trust issues secret. I was being dishonest and felt sad and withdrawn.

At that time in the United States, Co-Counseling was taught in a once-a-week-for-sixteen-weeks format with a break after the eighth week. After the eighth class I spoke to Barbara about my fears and their impact on me. She stated emphatically I should not continue unless I was willing to voice my concerns to the class. She felt it would be a great opportunity for me to be honest and for her to discuss the importance of trusting in confidentiality. I thought about what she said but could not find the courage to speak my truth in front of Diane. If I did she would know I didn't trust her and, as silly as it seems now, would no longer like me.

I told Barbara I had to quit the training. She accepted my decision and directed me to another course in a town 25 miles away that also had just finished its eighth class. She called the trainer, told him about me, and asked if he would let me into the class. Considering my issues with trust, she told me I had been brave just showing up. Part of me simply wanted to quit, but with Barbara's encouragement I agreed to continue with the training in the other course She gave me the trainer's name and phone number, told me to call him in a couple of days, and then she gave me a big hug.

Chapter 7

Walking into a New Class

I wake into this day
It will unfold as it unfolds
I plan . . . and . . . life happens

One of the trainers in the new class, Paul, was a member of my men's group, and this made it easy for me to talk about my experience in the other class. He listened without comment and told me he had a long conversation with Barbara, who felt I was ready to do some big work. He was very welcoming. I was nervous.

The class was held in the basement of a church that lacked the intimacy of Barbara's living room, but when the people is the class joined hands creating the opening circle, I felt connected. In the circle Paul simply introduced me as someone who had taken the first eight weeks of the training with another teacher and wanted to experience the training in a different class. We went around the opening circle several times with people saying how they felt having a new person in their class. I said I was glad to be here. Each time we went around the circle I felt more and more included as a member of the class.

Although a bit nervous, I felt safe in this class. My thinking was that none of these people knew me or anyone in Barbara's class. The anonymity made confidentiality seem more secure. This sense of safety excited me. I felt ready to learn what there was to learn and be honest about my life.

That night the class worked with the concept of *patterns* and *pattern* formation. I remember Paul saying in a loud booming voice, "Get it, patterns are real. They impact us every day. They are real! They are not bad or good. They are natural. The only question is: Do they serve you or don't they serve you?"

Patterns, as used in Co-Counseling, are similar to habits. Many are learned while we are young without us being conscious we are actually learning anything. They are acquired by repetitive actions in response to certain situations. They consist of thoughts, feelings, and behaviors. They seem so familiar to us that we think "that is just the way we are." All of our patterns, however, are learned and run involuntarily. In this way they are like computer programs—once you hit the key to initiate them, they will start running and will continue to run until they are done. Patterns are triggered by words, thoughts, or actions similar to the situations in which they were originally acquired and will normally run till they are done. Most patterns serve us while others don't. (For a fuller explanation of patterns see Chapter 20.)

"What we learned as children to survive keeps us from living as adults" is an expression I learned in the twelve-step program Adult Children of Alcoholics. Patterns run without our conscious consent. Identifying patterns is not easy, and creating new ways of responding to the situations in which patterns normally occur is even more difficult. Paul said examining patterns would be the focus of the work we would do in the training, and would be a major part of the work we will do as self-counselors for as long as we cocounsel. He emphasized that only after you truly start believing patterns are real will you start seeing them and create alternatives to them.

Children learn by repetition, whether it is walking up stairs or not speaking unless spoken to. We tend to hold on to what we learn, especially if it worked. Our lives change as we grow older and just because a particular patterned response worked for us in the past does not

37

mean it is appropriate in the present. But we run the pattern anyway because it is an automatic, unconscious response to a situation that in some way resembles a situation from our past. So, patterns are triggered. The important work in moving our lives forward is to identify patterns and the triggers that engage them.

Here in the class, I was being challenged to identify patterns and the triggers that engage them and start them running. We were encouraged to make a direct connection between how the triggers in the present resemble the original situations in the past that we reacted to, thus creating the pattern.

I left Barbara's course to get away from Diane so I could *do my work*, but what happened in the course followed me into the new training. As Paul explained the concept of patterns, all I could think of was Diane and the conflict and agitation that drove me from Barbara's course. As I thought about Diane and myself, I began to realize that my behavior around her was similar to how I had acted around other women, indicating that a deeply engrained pattern was involved.

I started thinking of my childhood when Paul told us to pair up to do a session. He wanted us to identify a pattern we recently ran, or, as he said, "ran us" but didn't serve us. He told us to search back in our lives and find the origins of the pattern.

Here, as if by some magical coincidence, I was presented with the opportunity to explore what went on for me in Barbara's class using this framework of patterns, which shined a new light on my behavior and what lay behind it. When I paired up, I said I wanted to go first. I immediately started exploring the turmoil and conflict that dominated my thinking for the past several weeks. The framework allowed me to do this without making myself bad or wrong. The shame I felt about my behavior began to disappear as I began to see my actions as based in patterns that had been active my whole life.

Chapter 8

Patterns Are Real

Walking through muck of day
Keep going . . .
Appreciate the muck
Then muck becomes dance floor

The training was designed for us to learn how to be skilled cocounselors. We were taught techniques and skills, conceptual frameworks within which to work, and ways to bring what we learned directly into our lives. There were wonderful discussions about the human spirit and the resilience of being human. The training was filled with a buoyancy and belief in the goodness of people and the possibility of creating a life filled with love, joy, and creativity. Mostly it was experiential. We did session work and group sharing. Each class began with an opening circle and ended with a closing circle. In these circles we had the time to look at, see, and appreciate each other.

I was glad I had switched classes. In the new class I explored what had happened in Barbara's class, and to my great relief, I did not feel judged. When I did paired work, I was not afraid to speak truthfully about what I was thinking, doing, or feeling and sometimes even allowed myself to express my emotions. I always felt safe with, and heard by my session partner. I started to think my life wasn't as hopeless as I thought when I left Barbara's course.

I identified six or seven separate patterns that shaped my behavior and thinking in the prior class. I even began seeing patterns within and among these patterns. I also started remembering other times in my life when these same patterns had a direct bearing on my actions. Together they seemed to form a web that repeatedly snared me and kept me in crisis. I ended up focusing on a single pattern that seemed to be at the center of the web.

All my troubles in the first training began when Diane walked in. She was one of my supervisors. She had power over me. I leaped to the similarity between her and the nuns from the Catholic elementary schools I had attended. To *young* Fred these nuns were not to be trusted. They seemed arbitrary in dispensing punishment, of which I received a disproportionate share. They would call my mother and tell her I was disrupting the class and causing problems. When I got home, my mother would punish me because of what the nuns said. She always seemed to take the word of the nuns or anyone else who had something bad to say about me. I never felt like she listened to me when I tried to tell her my side of what happened. I think I transferred some of this mother stuff onto Barbara and unconsciously thought she would not protect me if it came down to some issue between Diane and me. Was this why I only told her about my problems after I had decided to leave the class?

As a young boy I had learned not to trust women, especially if they had any power over me. I explored where else this pattern showed up and was not surprised to find it had negatively impacted all my relationships with women. I was scared of women and, in my fear, was always tentative and looking for approval. I had an easy time working on these issues when I was paired with a man but struggled to examine these same issues with a female partner. Near the end of the training I was paired with a women and decided to work on my trust issues with women. She did not run away or halt the session. She gave me her full attention and a hug when my turn as the self-counselor was done. Her apparent acceptance of me as being all right after what I had shared was a big deal to me. In the sharing circle following the session I said what I had done and stated it was a breakthrough for me to say in the presence of a woman that I had a deeply in-grained pattern of not trusting women. Despite speaking this truth out loud in front of women, my world did not fall apart, and I realized the pattern had shifted.

I remember driving home after each class thinking how complex everyone's life is. All the people in the course were dealing with fascinating, complex issues. I was particularly amazed at how ready the trainers were to share the issues and problems in their lives. Their willingness to be open and honest gave everyone in the training permission to talk freely about what was going on in their lives. I admired the honesty being spoken and the expression of emotions that often accompanied the honesty. I recognized how brave all these people were to confront the issues in their lives. Co-Counseling gives people the forum to do that and be in charge of their own exploration.

Chapter 9

Feeling Safe

Caress your warm soft heart
Appreciate your deep sadness
Then love feeling alive

On the 25-mile drive to class I could feel my body relaxing. In the new class I had no fear of being judged negatively, being ridiculed, or having what I said come back at me in some twisted way. I was learning a great lesson about the importance of feeling safe. Most of my life I had not felt safe. I had lived in fear of others' judgments, and as a result did not feel free to express myself or give my opinion. My lack of safety was so pervasive that I accepted it as normal.

The origins of this pattern lay in the persistent criticism I faced from my mother and the nuns. The trigger was, sadly, any time I opened my mouth to express an opinion or personal thought. I did express my views, but deep inside me I expected that whatever I said would be negated and that I would end up feeling stupid. Despite my doctoral degree, I lived in the expectation that my ideas would be rejected, and in the rejection of my ideas was a rejection of me.

One of the last things Barbara said to me when I told her I was leaving the class was that I needed to pay attention to my issues around safety and trust. In the new class, any time I felt fear I thought of her words and examined my sense of safety. I realized I was feeling safe in this church basement. It was the first time in my life I ever consciously sensed I was safe in a group of people—another step forward.

I was developing a deep faith that, no matter what I did or said, I would be supported. In this embracing safety, I felt free to be totally and completely me. I was surprised and delighted at my own spontaneity and exuberance. I felt accepted and safe with everyone in the class, and this even made it easy for me to reclaim being silly, a sensation I had lost somewhere in my childhood.

Outside of class I found it hard to talk about the training, especially the patterns and issues I was working on. I could talk about all of this in my men's group, but outside of that group, there was no one with whom I could share this important work. So as much as I loved being honest in the training and in my men's group, I was growing distant from the people I had called friends. I did not trust them to accept me if I shared with them the intense internal work I was doing or the joy the work was bringing me.

My admiration for the people in the training soared as I was privileged to hear about the reality of their lives. I had never been a confidant of anyone. These people were maintaining their everyday lives while working on difficult, life-changing issues. I was fascinated with their stories and wanted to tell the world about them but could not because of rules of confidentiality.

I gradually began to realize that confidentiality, as practiced in Co-Counseling, required true discipline. Holding confidentiality went against the fabric of social conversation, which, all too often, involves discussing other people's problems but not our own. I found it hard not to jump into a conversation when I could add a juicy tidbit I had heard in my role of co-counselor. I kept catching myself as I began to tell a story from the class that seemed like it could add to a conversation. Part of me said the people I was with knew no one in my class so it would be all right to share what they were working on, but I stayed aware of confidentiality and maintained silence. During these weeks I was training my brain to be disciplined. Every time I stopped myself from sharing someone else's story, I was honoring my commitment to the members of the class and to Co-Counseling. By the time the training was ending I knew I could hold confidentiality. I felt a sense of strength that I was disciplined enough to hold a firm boundary. I was worthy of these peoples' trust.

As the training progressed and we learned more skills and techniques designed to help us explore our internal world, I applied everything to the work I was doing on patterns. I was fascinated using this concept as a basis for examining my life. I started questioning just about everything I did. Was I in pattern, unconsciously reacting to what was happening in the present, or was I consciously processing the current situation as a unique experience? I still liked my instincts, but even here I did more exploration than I used to before proceeding. I wanted clarity about what I was doing and how I was doing it.

One specific thought began to trouble me. In my thinking about Diane, I never entertained the idea that she might have changed. I had her locked into being exactly who she was several years ago and never conceived of the possibility that she might have grown, become more conscious, and stopped gossiping. I wanted to know why I hadn't considered that. The answer I kept coming up with was that deeply imbedded in me was a pattern that said, "people don't change." I was working to change, but a part of me did not believe change was possible.

47

I brought the question of change to my men's group, and we had a great discussion. What I remember is someone saying we are all organic beings, and everything organic grows and changes. Thus we are always changing—it was perfectly normal to change. I now had a solid concept that contradicted my "no one changes" pattern. Every organism changes, and humans are organic beings. Everybody could change, including Diane, whom I had vilified. She might well have changed, but because of the pattern, I could not even conceive of that possibility. I was now becoming more conscious of myself, and the realization of this growing consciousness meant I was changing; and if I could change, then everybody could change. I was waking up.

Chapter 10

Bringing Co-Counseling Home

I know now what I want
It scares me into alertness
Each step is important

As I drove home after each class I reviewed new skills, contemplated new insights, and planned how to implement goals I set for myself. My life was moving in a positive direction, and the spirit of the training stayed with me for most of the ride home. The critical voices in my brain started speaking their doubts as I got closer to my house and by the time I pulled into the driveway I felt deflated. The voices said I was wasting my time and should be taking better care of my daughter and figuring out how to make more money. I felt weak in face of these daily problems. I spoke about all this extensively in my men's group, and they kept saying, "give it time." I now know change does not happen overnight. It requires vigilance, and it is not easy.

The eight-week training ended with lots of hugs and warmth. I was glad I had taken it and was proud of myself for completing the full course. I set up weekly sessions with a member of my men's group when the training ended. We worked in the loft in my apartment. I found it difficult, however, to stay clearly focused on my work in my own space. It was one thing to do sessions in a class while everyone else was doing them, but to do the paired work in my own home seemed strange. In the empty house the silence seemed to echo my words, giving them a hollow feeling I did not like. Doing sessions outside of the course seemed weird. I wasn't a therapist. This wasn't a therapist's office. This was my house, where all my problems dwelled. I doubted these sessions could help me.

I kept remembering Barbara and Paul saying Co-Counseling is a practice, however, and to get the real benefits from it you have to do regular sessions. My session partner insisted we continue, and I got strong encouragement to keep doing sessions from the men's group. After a time I regained the belief that the sessions were benefiting me. Working in the same place all the time was important. The space became special, and I started placing objects with personal meaning in this space. After a while the loft became my place to cocounsel. Doing sessions in my home started feeling natural, and the silence, which at first seemed to provide an empty echo for my words, now seemed to embrace my session partner and me. As I became more comfortable, I began feeling better after every single session.

In my sessions I was learning to look at myself from a place of centered awareness where I could see how I engaged the world. I started developing ideas about who I was—ideas that were different from those I formed growing up. I was taking responsibility for my actions and myself. I began to see and understand how things I did to survive in my childhood were keeping me from living fully in the present. As my awareness of myself changed, I changed.

I always had things to work on. I had emotions to release and released them. I took time to validate myself and celebrate what was new and good in my life. I began digging into my past to uncover the source of those patterns I became aware of and wanted to change. The sessions were working. I was becoming my own therapist.

One aspect of these sessions made me giddy. They were free. I remember paying the two therapists from whom I got so little. Now I paid nothing. I provided my Co-Counseling partner a service by being his co-counselor as he did his work, and he was my co-counselor when I was doing my work. In essence we bartered our time giving each other *caring-aware-attention* and the promise of confidentiality. And the space was free and becoming more beautiful all the time.

Chapter 11

The Power of Listening

Too many people can underestimate the value of just listening. It can be more helpful than anything a person might say.

—Ann Landers

About six months after the course ended, something happened that persuaded me to take the Fundamentals training again. At my job people started talking to me in ways they had never talked to me before. They were sharing intensely intimate details about their lives. I walked away from these conversations unsure of why they had shared what they shared. At a bar I frequented, I found myself at small tables with people telling me about personal matters I had not inquired about.

After about three weeks, I got it. One of the people talking to me said she trusted me because I was willing just to listen to her. I remembered Barbara saying that giving caring-aware-attention to a person would change the nature of your relationship with the person. She was right. I was listening with the caring-aware-attention I had learned in the Co-Counseling training, and my relationships were changing.

Caring-aware-attention was the baseline responsibility of the co-counselor. It involved caring for a person and holding him as good to the core of his being. It involved being fully aware of the person as he did his work—the tone of his voice, any movements of his body, the adjectives he used, and so much more. Giving caring-aware-attention also meant not judging the person, evaluating what he said, or attempting to fix him. It simply meant being *out with* the person so he could feel your positive energy.

Having a person sitting right across from me giving me his full caring attention was magical. The steadiness and softness of the eye contact that was maintained while giving caring-aware-attention gave me a sense of being safe, truly safe. I didn't get this feeling from the two therapists I saw, but did get it from Deborah. Receiving it felt like I was being watched over and cared for at the same time. Giving this attention is a wonderfully supportive way of listening.

Giving caring-aware-attention was the key to my newfound popularity. I had learned it during the training.

Now without any conscious thought, I brought it into my everyday life. I was now listening to people as I had never done before. Listening in this manner felt like a meditation to me. I was meditating on other people, paying complete attention without judging what they said or did. I stayed focused on them, breathing evenly, and feeling love for them as they shared their lives.

I touched something in these people by giving them soft direct eye contact and my full attention. This heart-centered, supportive listening is something they never got in normal social conversation. I simply listened to people. I did not interrupt them. I did not blush or get angry or seem agitated no matter what they shared. I gave them lots of room to say whatever they needed to say. Somehow just this simple listening technique seemed to give people permission to be honest.

Something special was going on for me. I started to feel wanted. People wanted to talk with me and, talk to me they did. They trusted me with what they shared without ever asking me not to repeat it. The compassion I exhibited, and strength with which I listened, seemed to be all they needed. People thanked me for "talking" to them, when in reality they were thanking me for listening to them. And as they told me about their lives I started feeling better about mine. I wasn't the only person with issues, doubts, and problems, even among my friends in the bar.

I did lots of listening and still do. When people finished talking about what they wanted to talk about and I started talking, however, they would interrupt me with stories or start telling me what I should do. They had no sense of how to give caring-aware-attention. I found it distressing but put up with it just to feel that people wanted to talk with me. It was important for me just to feel wanted.

Take Time to Listen, Not Talk

When I ask you to listen to me,
    and you start giving me advice,
    You have not done what I asked.
When I ask you to listen to me,
    and you begin to tell me why I shouldn't feel that
    way,
    You are trampling on my feelings.
When I ask you to listen to me,
    and you feel that you have to do something
        to solve my problems,
    You have failed me, strange as that may seem.

Listen:

All that I ask is that you listen.
Not talk or do—just hear me.

THE POWER OF LISTENING

When you do something for me that I need to do for
myself,
> you contribute to my fear and feelings of
> inadequacy.
But when you accept as a simple fact that I do feel what
I feel,
> no matter how irrational,
Then I can stop trying to convince you
> and go about the business of understanding
> > what's behind my feelings.
So, please listen and just hear me
And, if you want to talk,
Wait a minute for your turn -
> and I'll listen to you

—*Anonymous*

Chapter 12

Learning about Emotions

Explore your life today
Look into your heart
. . . into your soul . . .
Know always you are whole

The things I was learning about myself in Co-Counseling were not taught in schools. I was learning about my gut, my emotions, and my life. The basic emotions of sadness, fear, anger, and joy were discussed at length in the training. When we were asked where we felt them in our bodies, I was amazed people knew. One person felt anger in her hands, while others felt it in their bellies. Sadness came to peoples' awareness in their throats or behind their eyes. Fear seemed more random, but most people agreed their bodies became tense and their breath shallow. People in the class had a real sense of where they felt each emotion. I had no idea where I felt them. They were simply inside me.

Learning About Emotions

I remember a question Barbara asked that stumped the class: *What positive things were said about emotions in your childhood?* We looked at each other expectantly, but no one came up with anything. Just talking about emotions made me nervous. I was not allowed to have my emotions as a child or young person. I had an active temper and was repeatedly told it was bad and destructive and would get me in trouble. Sadness meant tears, and tears were for girls. I could never mention being scared because acknowledging fear in any way meant I would be labeled as weak and a 'scaredy-cat'. Joy simply did not exist in my young life. I seemed to laugh at the wrong times and would be pounced on with the accusing question, "What are you laughing at?" In my childhood, emotions were a black hole that sucked me into trouble. They needed to be avoided, and avoidance led to suppression.

In the Co-Counseling training I began to engage my emotions, especially anger, which had been suppressed my whole life. Looking back from the safety of the class, I saw that as a child my anger came out only as destructive rage. My anger frightened me. We did control loosening exercises in the training to wake up the different emotions within us. We engaged our emotions by acting as if we were mad, sad, scared, or joyous. When it came time to act into anger, Barbara got down on her knees in front of a pile of pillows and started pounding the pillows with her fists and yelling while she pounded. She was physically tired when she finished, but what I really noticed was the serene smile on her face. Every one took turns kneeling in front of the pillows and pounding as forcefully as they could. Barbara had to encourage some people to begin by first having them tap the pillows lightly with their fists to get them started. Some people screamed while they pounded, while others were silent.

I was the last person and was almost paralyzed as I knelt in front of the pillows. I couldn't move. Barbara encouraged me to strike the pillows, telling me it was safe and I would be okay. Finally she physically separated my hands, which were clenched together in front of me, and then laid them down on the pillows and left them there. She then said something about lifting them off the pillows. I don't remember what happened next, but I started pounding and then I was exhausted and started crying. I felt like a fool and after some time passed Barbara asked me if I was all right. I simply sat there totally lost.

She then used a technique called *present time,* which is designed to bring a person back to the present moment after finishing a session. After a bit I came back into my body. She asked me to look around and say peoples' names. I stumbled on a couple, and she had me do it again before I returned to my place in the circle. We then did a sharing round and I talked about my childhood issues with anger.

Learning About Emotions

Emotional-release work is an essential part of the Co-Counseling Fundamentals training. Both Barbara and Paul emphasized the importance of expressing, releasing, and discharging emotions whenever they came up in our sessions. The emotional release work in the course provided a safe place for me to open the gate to my emotions, which had been locked in my childhood. This accepting environment allowed me to stop being afraid to feel and express my emotions and to discover there was nothing to fear from them.

In my weekly sessions I engaged emotional issues using the techniques learned in the training. I was a storehouse of repressed emotions and in each session spent at least some time discharging these stored emotions. Releasing them gave me more and more energy for living my life. Gaining this new zest for life helped me free myself from old, negative, and limiting images of myself. I was taking charge of my life and liked who I was becoming.

During the next three years I paid particular attention to my emotions. In the safety of my paired work I discharged lots of anger and a surprising amount of sadness. I gradually came to accept emotions as neither good nor bad. As I let out the old repressed emotions, I became able to experience emotions as distinct from each other. I began to notice when I felt sadness, anger, fear, or joy and where these emotions showed up in my body, which was coming alive in new ways. The aliveness empowered me to start becoming friends with my emotions.

I remember Paul saying we needed to make friends with our emotions, and when we did, they would serve us well. I started to understand that having an emotional reaction to the world was normal. I was learning that I did not have to act on these gut reactions but simply to pay attention to them. They were becoming a second source of information for me to explore in my daily life along with the rational information gathered by my brain.

Chapter 13

Expanding My World

New beginnings explode
With simplest declarations
Be bold
step out of line

During the 1970s, before collapsing emotionally and finding Co-Counseling, I was an avid reader of Carlos Castaneda's books about Don Juan Matos, a Yaqui medicine man and sorcerer.[3] They fascinated me. Was the world Castaneda described real, or was it complete fiction? I wanted to believe it was real, and when I was reading the books, they were real. I could visualize Don Juan's house at the edge of the high desert somewhere in Mexico. I walked with the characters as they went on adventures in an arid land I had never experienced. There were some concepts about being human I wanted to believe, and I was fascinated with the concept of *non-ordinary* reality, which posited a universe beyond conventional Western thought. I found the adventures Carlos undertook under the guidance of Don Juan to be mysterious and exciting. These books had ideas I never seen written anywhere else. I wanted to believe there was more to life than I had experienced.

When I began Co-Counseling, I particularly liked the idea that, while I was in the self-counselor role, no one told me what to do or how to do it. I could use any ideas I wanted to help me explore and move my life. While I was cocounseling weekly, I started using Don Juan's conception of fear as an ally. He kept telling Carlos, who had become one of his apprentices, that fear would show him where he needed go next in his life. The process is quite simple. Look around your life; what most fascinates you and also brings up the most fear? This is where you need to go. *Follow your fear* was the message I took from Don Juan. I used it in my sessions to guide me.

In the winter of 1988–89, Michael, at a men's-group meeting, started talking about a Co-Counseling International workshop to be held in Hungary in the summer of 1989. When I heard this, I immediately wanted to go. The idea seemed totally outrageous. I had never traveled outside the United States except to Canada and a day trip to Tijuana, Mexico. I spoke only English, yet it seemed like I was destined to go. The truth was, I was terrified about going; and the more terrified I felt, the louder Don Juan's words about fear spoke to me. I wasn't even sure where

Hungary was. I knew the Soviet Union was breaking apart and Russian troops would soon be leaving Eastern Europe, including Hungary. It was a time of dramatic political upheaval, and although my only knowledge of Hungary was the 1956 Hungarian uprising against the Russians, I romanticized this country as mysterious.

I spent lots of session time considering the workshop in Hungary. I realized that, except for a generalized caution about the unknown, all my fears about going rested in the details—getting a passport, booking a flight, not knowing anyone, not knowing the language, not truly understanding why I wanted to go. I faced each of these fears, and as I did, each one dissolved. They became challenges and opportunities for me to be confident and vibrant. Using Don Juan's idea that fear is an ally, I moved through my fears and was set to go.

Michael, who had become a good friend, was excited I wanted to go. He, however, strongly suggested I attend the International Co-Counseling workshop to be held in the United States about 20 miles from where I lived. I knew of the gathering but had always chosen not to go, using the care of my daughter as an excuse. She had now moved out on her own, so I no longer had that excuse. I went and I'm glad I did because all my fears about who I was and my issues about being accepted all came to the surface before and during the workshop.

I felt out of place immediately. The workshop had ten women for every man and was clearly run by women, and Diane was there. In the first exercise during the opening circle, we were to wander around and introduce ourselves to other people and ask for a hug. Most of the people knew each other. I felt alone. Everyone was wandering around laughing, connecting, and giving each other long Co-Counseling hugs. I had grown fond of giving and receiving hugs so when I noticed a woman with a quiet smile on her face, I went up to her, said who I was, and asked for a hug. She looked at me with glaring eyes and said; "I don't hug men!" (We have subsequently become close friends, and although I remember the incident, she doesn't.)

I have limited memories of the workshop except I survived. I felt most comfortable with the few men who were there and some of the Europeans I met. I talked extensively with two women from Hungary. They were warm and friendly and spoke English; however when I cocounseled with them, they spoke Hungarian, which surprised me. I had cocounseled with people only in English and was amazed I could be fully present for them even though I did not understand what they were saying, and I found that I could do my work not knowing if they understood me. The more I talked with them, the more certain I was about going to the Co-Counseling International (CCI) European workshop in Hungary. By the end of the workshop I had filled out a registration form and paid a deposit. I was now fully committed to going and knew it was a big deal because of the intensity of the excitement and fear I had in my body.

Chapter 14

Into the Unknown

Each day begins
holding the life
we are destined to live

. . .

Don't believe yesterday

So in the summer of 1989 I flew to Vienna, met some American cocounselors, toured Vienna, and got on a bus into Hungary. The Austrian-Hungarian border was scary with guard towers, cement barriers, barbed wire, and long pole gates that were lifted to let the bus pass through. Two soldiers entered the bus and examined our passports. It took a long time for each American to explain why he or she was going into Hungary. The soldiers eventually left the bus, much to my relief, and we passed into Hungary. In the flat grassy fields immediately behind the barriers were hundreds of East Europeans camping and waiting for the day the Russians would leave so they could pass freely into Western Europe.

The air was electric with excitement and anticipation of the Russians leaving. Hungary would soon be free of foreign domination. The excitement spread into the workshop, which was held in an ancient castle on the Western Hungarian plains in a small town called Egervár. Every day began with an opening circle held outside the castle beneath one of the large yellowish walls. Sometimes we had to shout to be heard. The 150 of us held hands and ritually opened our day with a song or greeting, most of them in Hungarian but translated into English and Dutch.

This, like the international workshop I went to in America, was self-generating; meaning the people in attendance presented all the workshops. There were workshops geared toward releasing emotions and understanding patterns, an American led a workshop on self-validation; an Irishman led another on storytelling. Early in the morning people led workshops on yoga, tai chi and morning meditation. At night we danced, sang, and told stories. One evening we had an amazing talent show in the courtyard of the castle. The meals were raucous affairs, and I found myself eating strange foods. My palate was being challenged. Each day at the opening circle all the workshops and other activities being planned for the day were presented and explained. Some people went sightseeing in Egervár and other local towns. The old castle rocked with laughter and the sounds of joyous people celebrating life.

My Journey Into Co-counseling

I had a birthday during this time and, as a conscious birthday present to myself, offered a "rebirthing" workshop.[4] I had never led a workshop. My rebirthing teachers kept telling me I had the knowledge, experience, and skill to lead one, but I was too insecure. At the Hungarian Workshop I had nothing to lose. Only a handful of people knew me so I figured even if the workshop was a bust I would not be disgraced. I was scared to do it, but again listening to Don Juan's advice, I followed my fear and did it. I carefully planned all aspects of the workshop, asked Michael to assist me, announced the workshop at an opening circle, and posted a sign up sheet, which, to my surprise, was immediately filled to overflowing. It was a five-hour workshop and a great success. As word of the workshop spread, I was asked to run it again, and I did. It was as powerful as the first workshop. A Dutch cocounselor still remembers exactly what happened in it, as do I. About half the participants at the gathering took it, and because of its success, I was asked to lead the closing circle and said *yes*.

The last night arrived with a sense of excitement and anticipation. A huge full moon dominated the clear sky bathing the earth in a brilliant silvery light. We gathered around a blazing bonfire outside the walls of the old castle. We were 150 women, men, and children, arm in arm, singing traditional Hungarian songs; then someone

70

started singing "We Shall Overcome" in English. Most people joined in adding verses appropriate to what was happening in Hungary as well as verses from the American civil rights movement. Flames soared 30 feet into the air as our voices thundered into the night. Swaying in harmony with our singing, we stared at each other's brightly lit, smiling faces. The organizers came into the center of the circle, and we all cheered. The flames subsided, and I stepped forward and invited everyone to raise their eyes to the moon. After a lingering pause, I asked that whenever cocounselors gather under a full moon, they remember this first Hungarian CCI workshop and tell the story of this land and this gathering. As my words were translated into Hungarian and Dutch, the circle grew tighter and quieter.

The fire had collapsed onto itself, burning with a blue-red flame, when people began to leave the circle and disappear into the castle. Many of us didn't want to leave. I didn't want to leave. I had found a new home where I had the courage to stand up and be seen as knowledgeable and strong. As the circle grew smaller and smaller, we, swaying to some shared felt rhythm, moved closer and closer to the fire's glowing embers. The moonlight poured down on us from a black sky. We gradually ceased swaying. Protected from the wind by the walls of old castle, silence enveloped us as we watched the glow of the dying fire. Standing in the stillness, I felt the stirrings of a new beginning moving through me. I had changed. Now I had the conscious freedom to be the creator of my own life. This night in Egervár would stay alive in me as the end of the cycle that began with the night of my emotional collapse. I was beginning the next part of my life.

Chapter 15

A Kitchen Table Conversation

Treasure your sacredness
Create space
to
honor the divine
Life unfolds perfectly

After the workshop ended I went to Budapest where local cocounselors graciously hosted many of us from different countries. We would meet each morning at the Café Gerbeaud, which lies in the heart of the city. One morning an energetic Hungarian cocounselor, István, gave myself and another American a guided tour through the alleys of the old castle district, around where he lived. As we walked the narrow cobblestone streets, he told us tales of marauding Huns from the 9th century and the rise of St. Stephen, the patron saint of Hungary. We visited the cathedral built in St. Stephen honor. Our guide showed us bullet holes in the ancient walls from modern times and talked about the 1956 uprising against the Russians. After about two hours he stopped outside two massive wooden doors and invited us into the apartment he shared with his mother. He unlocked a small door, and we stepped into a small cobblestone courtyard. We climbed some stairs and entered a dimly lit apartment of large rooms with high ceilings, old paintings on the walls, and ornate furniture. The curtained windows on the opposite side of the apartment from where we entered overlooked the Danube River flowing through the heart of the city.

After looking around the apartment István's mother, a doctor who had lived through the Russian occupation as well as the German occupation before that, invited me to join her for tea in the modernized kitchen. She was fluent in English and spoke with a strong voice filled with confidence and knowing. She had become a doctor when women were subjugated and had survived hostile environments since her teenage years. She asked me, who I was, what I was doing in Hungary, and what I planned to do when I returned to America. We drank tea as I went through my story. I finished by telling her about my growing commitment to Co-Counseling including my newfound desire to become a trainer. She asked me more questions about Co-Counseling and I explained it to her the best I could. It was clear my explanation did not satisfy her.

She wanted to know about the beliefs that created the foundation upon which Co-Counseling was built as well as the cultural norms that sustained it. I had never really thought about either of these questions and told her so. She grew agitated. How could I commit myself to something without knowing what the basic beliefs and cultural norms were? I told her I knew about the process and skills people used in the practice of Co-Counseling, but had never thought about the underlying beliefs or culture that supported it. I also knew that it worked for me, and being here in Hungary was proof that it worked.

"The beliefs and culture supporting your work and your life is what is really important" she asserted. "You Americans don't care about culture because you Americans don't have a culture and you don't really believe in anything. You just go merrily along doing, doing, doing," she said emphatically. "Your nation is too young. Hungary, on the other hand, has a culture that has sustained us through hundreds of years of foreign domination. People have conquered our land and our resources, but they have never been able to conquer us because we have our culture. The Hungarian people survive today as the Russians get out and we will not have changed because they occupied our country for the past 44 years. But our culture is so strong it limits our view of the future. It is a culture of survival and not growth. You Americans can grow because you don't have a fixed culture."

She was striking the table forcefully as she spoke. She kept telling me beliefs and culture are critical, and if I was to become a Co-Counseling teacher, I better know what they are and understand them. Pay attention to them because they have more of an impact on you and your Co-Counseling than you imagine and "you better get to know them before you become a teacher."

I felt speechless and only after she got up and refilled our teacups for the third time did I get chance to ask her about her life. I got little glimpses of her life as she talked. Little stories, mostly disconnected, which seemed more like fiction than reality. Here was a person who had survived and thrived while living her life under the domination of people she did not like and did not trust. She clearly paid attention to the specific world she lived in so she could prosper while also maintaining a powerful internal life. Culture, to her, is what sustains a people, an organization, or a religion no matter the trials or afflictions they may have to endure.

A Kitchen Table Conversation

When I left the apartment, I began thinking about the beliefs and culture of Co-Counseling. I had never met such a vigorous, passionate, intellectually sharp person before in my life, so I took what she said seriously. That conversation set me on a course of inquiry that ultimately led to the writing of this book.

Part II

Transition

Prologue

The trip to Hungary and the International workshop in Egervár was a trip into the unknown. I didn't know enough to anticipate any of what I would do or experience. My first day in Vienna I went into a cathedral, lured by a type of music I had never heard and inside, a man from California was playing the strange music on a synthesizer. He was studying music in Vienna, but every winter he spent with a tribe in Mexico recording their music. He was attempting to duplicate the music on his synthesizer.

My whole trip was like walking into that cathedral in Vienna. I expected to hear Bach, but heard Mexican tribal music played by a man from California. Everything was exciting and different. Even when I fully expected to find one thing, something else was there for me to discover. I went with a great deal of fear, which I kept walking through by taking Don Juan's advice, and I came home stronger and more vibrant than I had ever felt.

Chapter 16

The Chain Bridge

Transformation begins
In the most
unnoticed
small ways
then it becomes conscious

Shortly after my kitchen conversation with István's mother, I headed for the airport to return to the United States. Getting on the plane I felt like I was stepping out of a dream. I looked out the window at the soldiers on the tarmac and the sad physical condition of Ferihegy International Airport in Budapest and began appreciating the reality I had just experienced. A universe had opened for me in two weeks. Vienna and Budapest were no longer dots on a map but bustling cities of noise, colors, smells, and people. As I explored the streets of these cities, I grew beyond the small, insular Fred who got on an airplane in New York. In Budapest, after the CCI, I was totally open and drank in the mysterious environment of the city with its dark, coal-stained buildings and cobblestone streets. I shared a glorious, passionate kiss on the sidewalk outside a post office with a Hungarian woman with whom I am still in contact. I'd grown bigger and energetically stronger in ways I didn't really understand.

Standing on the Chain Bridge in the center of Budapest and watching the Danube flow on its journey to the Black Sea, I felt the world of European geography, politics, and history become tangible. This bridge, where the Nazis dumped bodies of Jews and Gypsies into the Danube, turning it into a river of blood, was built in 1849. It has carried scores of invading armies over this river that runs through the heart of Europe. The river carries the brutal, changing history of Europe in its waters. Standing there, I began to understand the importance for many European cocounselors to view Co-Counseling as both a means of personal growth and a means of social change. They were much closer to the realities of politics gone bad than I could ever be.

Walking the old cobblestone streets, looking into store windows, watching people, and exploring cathedrals older than the United States were only parts of the adventure. The international Co-Counseling community gathered in Egervár was a dazzling collection of characters seemingly created by fiction writers. Journalists, dancers, doctors, businessmen and women, mothers with their children, librarians, therapists—all, and more, were present. Many spoke English, so I had wonderful conversations and I learned about their lives, realities, and ways of being in the world that were remarkably different from each other's and mine. They embodied a freedom of expression and wildness I'd only experienced in the radical hippie days of the 1960s.

I had become aware of many differences between American and European thinking about the scope and impact of Co-Counseling. Europeans view Co-Counseling as a radical, transformational approach to personal and social development. Many saw this work as helping to build a more human world. The basis for this view is that, as individuals become healthier and more open, the society will become healthier and more open. So as people heal childhood wounds and become more conscious and creative, they naturally work to make the society more humane and caring. So Co-Counseling, by having a positive impact on individuals, has a positive impact on the larger society. In the United States I had never heard anyone talk about Co-Counseling impacting the larger society. Everything was couched in terms of purely personal healing and growth. This larger view of Co-Counseling excited me.

Looking out the window as the plane took off I felt deeply alive. The world I had experienced vibrated within me.

I had met and become friends with people from different European countries. I now had playmates I could learn from and play with. Not only had I survived in an unknown world, I had thrived. I wanted to cheer and celebrate my successful venture into the world.

Not only was I bringing back stories of people, places, and experiences, I was also bringing back my awakened self. I had caught the enthusiasm for life many European Co-Counselors seemed to possess. The man who was leaving Hungary did not have the same doubts and fears about himself as the man who boarded a plane in New York City and landed in Vienna. I was heading back to the United States with more confidence about my life. I had left my attitude of being merely a survivor in the soil of this ancient country where I had been accepted and seen as a strong, independent person. I was starting to appreciate myself, and the life I was living. I now saw myself as an adventurer and person of ideas. When the plane landed at JFK, I knew my life had changed.

Chapter 17

Stepping into
My New Life

There is only one way
to live our life with real passion
Walk
straight into your dreams

Back in the United States I was alive with the spirit of Co-Counseling. I was thrilled with the simple experience of being appreciated for who I was. At the workshop cocounselors from many nations worked and played together with enthusiasm. Everyone shared the basic tenants of Co-Counseling taught in the Fundamentals training, so there was a common understanding of how we did our work and a common language we used to communicate. The spirit of acceptance and community spiraled into an enthusiasm for life that soared as the days passed. I now held a vision of Co-Counseling as a planet-wide movement of loving people like those I had met in Hungary. I wanted to be part of this dynamo of human energy.

In Connecticut a community gathering was held to celebrate those of us who went to Hungary and to hear our stories. We all related our personal experiences. In my sharing I explained that, before going to Europe, I viewed Co-Counseling strictly in terms of my own personal work. Now I saw it as a global association of individuals committed to self-healing and growth while embracing personal change as the basis for community and societal change. I had learned a lot about myself on the trip. The success of my workshops and my facilitation of the closing circle added mightily to the whole experience. I had no idea what to expect when I left for Hungary, and I returned with gifts I had not known existed.

I then announced I wanted to become a Co-Counseling trainer. My life had changed dramatically for the better since I started Co-Counseling; now I wanted to embrace Co-Counseling as a major part of my life. I had never thought of becoming a trainer before my time in Hungary. Having experienced the impact this personal growth modality had on people in Europe, however, I now felt Co-Counseling was a radical, transformative process that could help make the world a better place one person at a time. I had been active in Co-Counseling for five years as a practitioner. It had helped me to deal with my emotional collapse and to recognize and change old, ingrained patterns, It had put me in the driver seat of my own life, which had become more stable because I no longer wasted energy battling with myself over every decision I made. I came back from the European Co-Counseling workshop with a new abundance of energy, and teaching Co-Counseling was an exciting outlet for this energy.

In Europe I had been surprised and inspired to find almost as many men as women at the workshop. In the United States there were hardly any men in Co-Counseling. I felt the positive experience I had with the men in my men's group would serve me in teaching men this set of techniques and skills. I was going to bring Co-Counseling to men. I knew I thrived in the positive environment of my men's group and in the total acceptance I felt within Co-Counseling circles. To bring these two places of positive growth together seemed natural.

Chapter 18

From Apprentice to Trainer

To be strong when you act
Know exactly what you desire
Then proceed with passion

I still had a lot to learn about Co-Counseling. I knew it only from a practitioner's perspective. Somewhere in my past I had heard: If you want to really learn something, teach it. I was determined to learn everything about Co-Counseling—the process, techniques, and skills involved, the history of the organization and how it worked, as well as the beliefs and culture that sustains it. I apprenticed with two experienced trainers who were very different from one another. The first person had an extensive syllabus, which she gave me before the training began and told me to study it. We would meet two or three days before each class and go over the exercises and skills to be taught in that class. She made sure

87

I understood the theory behind the exercises we would be teaching and then would have me model them for her. In class she taught while I observed her and the people in the training. After each class she asked me how I thought each student was doing, how the pieces we taught fit together with the rest of the material we had covered, and if I had any questions about what she had done in the class. Near the end of the training she started asking me to explain particular points and to answer questions.

In my second apprenticeship, I developed the syllabus and did most of the teaching. The teacher and I would meet one hour before each class, and I would tell her what I was going to do in that class. Basically, she asked me why I was going to do what I was going to do and how it built on what had gone before. She sat in the class and observed me in the role of trainer. On occasion she would clarify a point, answer a question, or ask me a really tough question in front of the class, persisting until I answered it to her satisfaction. After each class she would grade me on how I taught, how I handled questions, how I managed time, and how I interacted with the students. Mostly it was positive, but on occasion she would point out where and how I had lost control of the class or had been unclear in an explanation or in response to a question.

From Apprentice To Trainer

During these apprenticeships I realized that the essential factors for teaching Co-Counseling were my ongoing, regular practice of it and my ability to explain how I had used it to change my own life. Making the exercises and skills real inside the training relied on sharing how they worked; and because of confidentiality, the only person a trainer could tell tales about was himself. I was the model through which the power of Co-Counseling could be demonstrated. As an apprentice I learned the art of moving from the role of trainer to doing my personal work as another member of the class and then reassuming the role of trainer. I made the transition easily and was commended for it.

This is one of the things that separate Co-Counseling from any other class or training I had ever taken. In all my other classes there were the teachers and students. The teachers held the knowledge, and that knowledge separated them from the students. As the trainer in Co-Counseling it was my job to explain and model a technique, skill, or process and then to pair up with someone and practice that skill using my own life as the basis of my work just as everyone else in the class did. As trainer I joined in the sharing circle that followed every exercise and stated what the exercise did for me while also answering issues and questions from members of the training. So in Co-Counseling trainers are always seen both as trainers and as humans working truthfully on their lives like everyone else in the training.

I got the sense there was freedom for trainers to be themselves while they were teaching. The material covered in a 40-hour Fundamentals training was extensive, and individual classes could become intense. I learned about the inter-connectedness of the exercises, techniques, and skills that made up the heart of the Co-Counseling process. I learned, not only to value the input of everyone in the training, but also to see each person in the training as my teacher. I was devouring everything about Co-Counseling so I would become a competent trainer. I was also learning a lot about myself and was excited about the richness I was experiencing. I was consciously moving my life in a direction I wanted.

A year after I came back from Hungary I started teaching the 40-hour Co-Counseling Fundamentals training. My first class was held in the basement of the Unitarian Church in West Hartford, Connecticut. There were over twenty men in the class. I had developed a thirty-page syllabus detailing everything I did, from walking into the first class to walking out the door after the last class. I worked hard developing my syllabus, which closely followed and was strongly influenced by the syllabus of the first teacher I apprenticed with. I followed the syllabus's timing to the minute. It became a joke in the class when I would say we were now three minutes behind schedule. I made sure everything I was supposed to teach was taught. There was little room for questions or dialogue. I wanted the people in my trainings to know how to cocounsel, so I used every minute by either teaching or having them practice.

The training went well. People learned Co-Counseling, and I gained a deeper understanding of the skills taught and the exercises used in the course. I also acquired a new respect for the power of the process as I watched people change elements of their lives during the time of the training. Lastly I became more confident in myself, and my ability to teach as I completed each three-hour class in the training.

Chapter 19

Appreciating the magic

Where is the magical
but in the attitudes we hold

Believe in your magic

When I returned from Hungary, I came back ready for new adventures in living besides becoming a Co-Counseling trainer. At home I was rooted in my job, which was good, and my house, which was beautiful. Both, however, were in a small city where I no longer felt challenged. I wanted to see more of the world. My daughter was finding her way independent of me, so I felt free to consider all options. Within a year of returning I moved out of my house to live in a much larger, urban area and found a new job with new people and new challenges. I was moving into new worlds.

For the next ten years my life had two centers: Work and Co-Counseling. I took on more demanding jobs and got involved in my professional association, which involved travel and public advocacy. My jobs were frustrating and rewarding like most jobs. With their professional commitments, however they satisfied my desire to be political while providing me a decent income. Despite the demands of work, I consciously carved out time to teach at least two Fundamentals trainings a year. I also became more involved in the world of Co-Counseling by working with the New England organization and with a teacher's group. Within these two centers my life was an adventure every day, and I bounded into each day with purpose and energy.

My life as a Co-Counseling trainer was richly rewarding. I started feeling more and more comfortable with the material in the Fundamentals training. I no longer relied on my syllabus, as I had when I first taught. Over the years my courses started including women. These trainings were different from those with only men. They were less raucous and filled with many more questions requiring detailed explanations. In each training, regardless of the people in it, a powerful spirit of supportive community developed that was not part of any syllabus.

I taught the Fundamentals training in the same way I learned it with Barbara and Paul and had practiced it in my apprenticeships. There was practically no theory; in fact, there was no room for theory. I seldom mentioned beliefs or how exercises or practices were tied together as a coherent whole. I simply trained people to become cocounselors. I needed them to know about the two roles and what to do in them. The primary focus of my teaching was on the role of the self-counselor and the skills and techniques a person could use while in this role. People came to the training for many reasons, but underlying these reasons was a desire to explore some dis-ease in their lives and make changes that would alleviate the dis-ease. They did this work consciously in the role of the self-counselor, as the time spent in the training is heavily weighted toward that purpose. The role of the co-counselor is taught as a purely supportive witness, as I had experienced as a new student and as an apprentice. The role is critical to Co-Counseling being successful, but the elements of it are taught early in the training; thereafter, the focus centers on the work of the self-counselor.

There is a magical moment in each course when it changes from a training made up of individuals to a community of participants who care as much about supporting each other as they do about their own work. Not that people stop doing their own work; in fact, they seem to do it more intensely after this point is crossed. Several things happen to bring about this change. It begins during the exploration of the four basic emotions and a series of control-loosening exercises in which everyone gets the opportunity to "act into" each emotion. People in the

94

class physically move into a posture of sadness and then, making the sounds of sadness, let their bodies bring forth the emotion. The same is done with fear, joy, and anger. People shake out fear, laugh in a silly manner expressing their joy, and express anger by pounding pillows. By letting everyone else in the class see them being emotionally honest the participants's normal social barriers are lowered. It is as if they have seen each other naked.

People are surprised at how easy it is to call forth their emotions. For most of them, this is probably the first time they have ever had total permission to let out their emotions. We live in a non-cathartic society in which the expression of emotions is disapproved of as either a sign of weakness or a lack of control. The release of emotions, therefore, is a private affair hidden from the public. For the people in the class to freely express their emotions in front of each other breaks a societal taboo that keeps people separate and isolated, especially in times of personal crisis. These exercises break open the dynamics of people's relationships with each other.

Two other factors come into play as the magic of community grows in the class. People start becoming honest out loud. They give up any pretense of looking good or putting on airs. They become real in front of each other, and many times their honesty has an emotional expression that stirs a deep resonance within everyone in the class.

TRANSITION

It is hard to witness a person being honest without true compassion coming forth. This last factor may, in fact, be the keystone that brings everything else together. Each person in the class sits in the role of the co-counselor witnessing another person honestly exploring the pain, joy, uncertainty, and struggle all humans experience but seldom reveal. Participants start to understand that, while giving caring-aware-attention, their session partners are working on their lives in real time right in front of them. They start to appreciate that their session partners trust them with the intimate details of their lives and in turn, they extend the same trust when they are in the role of the self-counselor. Since people in a class pair up with different people for different exercises, everyone in the training sooner or later works with every other person. The level of trust that builds in a class is amazing and contributes to the shift from a group of separate individuals to a supportive community of energetic partners.

During these ten years, I also attended Co-Counseling workshops in the United States, Western Europe, and New Zealand. In many ways the same warmth and supportive acceptance occurred spontaneously in these gatherings as they do in a Fundamentals training. The supportive feeling of community and personal connection weaves its way into participants' interactions. The vibrant dynamics that develop in trainings are present in the gatherings. There was always a sense of being together as one integrated whole, which never existed in the professional conferences or workshops I use to attend. The interpersonal connections among people seem based in human compassion and acceptance, not polite handshakes and physical separation. In the daily opening circles everyone gets a chance to be seen while at the same time seeing the other people who make up the circle. People identify themselves by their first names only. There is no rank or power differential within the circle. Each person is an equal part of the whole. In the session work, which occurs from the beginning of the gatherings to the end, people have the opportunity to give and receive the warmth and joy of caring-aware-attention. The great delight of being part of the exceptional energy of a heart-based community lights up these international gatherings of cocounselors and makes them a beacon of hope and human connection in our individualistic, isolated world.

I began paying closer attention to what was happening in my trainings after two international meetings that stirred my interest. The first, held in Tuscany, Italy, focused on the place of the human spirit within Co-Counseling. At this meeting everyone agreed that the human spirit was engaged during the Fundamentals and was alive at all gatherings big and small, but exactly how it was engaged was a mystery. At this meeting I also got my first real taste of the theory underlying Co-Counseling. John Heron, who hosted the workshop, is a theoretical master who can tie together many concepts and ideas into a meaningful coherent whole. His work provides the conceptual framework to explain how and why the co-counseling process is so effective in moving peoples' lives. Understanding the theory provides a solid base for the practice, yet it is never apparent as individuals struggle with their lives nor with the magic of community that always happens when cocounselors gather.

The second meeting was held in Northern Fryslan, Netherlands, in the summer of 1998. It was an international teachers' meeting. One afternoon under the shadow of a windmill, teachers from around the world made a list on a roll of shelf paper of what they taught in their training courses. There was a general agreement about what was taught from conceptual ideas to practical exercises. Considering Co-Counseling has no central organization and is merely an informal cooperative of autonomous local networks, I think we all were amazed at how twenty-four years after the inception of this transformational process, everyone still agreed on basic concepts. Different names may be given to the ideas and exercises, but around the planet the central elements of Co-Counseling were remarkably the same.

If everyone was teaching the same material in basically the same way and everyone agreed that a human spirit was engaged during the Fundamentals training, then something remarkable was going on. I could see that whatever happened in the Fundamentals had a way of sustaining itself within the people who took the training because this spirit always manifested itself in a warm, accepting community whenever cocounselors gathered. Remembering my kitchen conversation from 1989, I started thinking about the importance of culture and that maybe a unique culture was being transmitted during the Fundamentals that lived within those who took the training.

With these thoughts about culture firmly fixed in my mind, I set out at the turn of the century to examine the culture that underlies Co-Counseling. I began my exploration knowing I felt safe and nurtured within the gatherings. There was no doubt in my mind cocounselors viewed each other as kindred beings. I was accepted, and I accepted others at the gatherings without knowing them. I started listening to the values and beliefs expressed by those deeply involved in Co-Counseling. It was clear immediately that Co-Counseling was not a religion because it did not require any gods, posit an afterlife, or concern itself with the origins or fate of the universe. Some people in it were deeply religious, but in different religions, others had no religious affiliation, while still others followed esoteric, mystical practices. All people spoke of these openly and freely. Having such diversity made for a rich pallet of ideas that constantly swirl around in Co-Counseling gatherings.

Part III

Culture

Prologue

Culture is a set of beliefs and practices flowing within and among a community of individuals uniting them into a viable whole. Culture manifests itself through the use of specialized language and a set of community norms. At the heart of Co-Counseling culture is the belief that all human beings are mysterious miracles capable of self-awareness, self-appreciation, and self-direction. Individuals need love, respect, and understanding as much as food and shelter to thrive during the human journey. The culture of Co-Counseling, with its emphasis on the individual as special and sacred, continually evolves. Co-Counseling is not static or secretive but is rather an open, transformational approach to personal development honoring the human body, mind, and spirit as an integral whole.

In this part of the book, I examine some of the major beliefs, behaviors, and practices shared by Co-Counseling communities around the planet.

Chapter 20

Some Beliefs about Being Human

Belief: Confidence in the truth or
existence of something not
immediately susceptible to rigorous proof.

— Random House
Dictionary

In my exploration of the culture of Co-Counseling, I repeatedly find a few simple, deeply embedded beliefs holding the culture in place. These beliefs are seldom acknowledged or articulated because the tangible, potent power of Co-Counseling lies in the actual experience. Like passengers on an airplane enjoying the benefits of flying without understanding the principles of flight, people can get the benefits of Co-Counseling without knowing the beliefs that support it. Naming these beliefs, however, brings greater clarity and understanding to why Co-Counseling's transformational approach to personal and social development has such inherent power.

All the practices and behaviors that have evolved during the forty years since the inception of Co-Counseling as a worldwide, self-counseling modality find their basis in these simple beliefs.

Belief #1: All of us are good to the core.

All humans are good to the core. Alternatives to this belief are that some people are good to the core while others are not, or no one is good to the core, or no core exists. Choosing to accept that *all people are good to the core* allows us to hold people in their goodness even when they are talking about something they have done that is harmful to themselves or others.

Belief #2: Emotions are the body's natural spontaneous reaction to either external events or internal expectations.

Emotions are physical events in the body. Each emotion has a distinct biochemical impact throughout the body and alters our experience of reality. The basic emotions of sadness, fear, disgust, anger, surprise, and joy have their own sets of biochemical actions influencing our physical and mental states of being.[5] Emotions are neither good nor bad, moral, nor immoral; they are simply part of our existence. We become friends with our emotions while working with them in the safe nest of Co-Counseling.

BELIEF #3: EACH OF US CREATED WHO WE ARE.

We learn to be who we are. We are not born with our adult personalities, beliefs, and ways of perceiving the world. On the most basic level a definite relationship exists between our physical body at birth (nature) and how we are raised (nurture). Being born female or male or as part of a minority or majority group within a majority dominated society (nature) greatly influences how we are raised (nurture). Just as learning to walk, climb stairs, ride a bicycle, or speak begins with, and continually uses, conscious effort over time, learning how to be who we are happens in the same way. We engage parents, siblings, and teachers; depending on their responses, we learn what works to get us what we want. We repeat the things that work over and over again and avoid the things that don't work.

The social responses that work for us as children become imbedded in our brain as neuro-networks and operate on an unconscious level in the same manner as our physical responses to our ordinary physical world. Thus when we have learned to climb stairs as children and a "stair climbing" neuro-network is imbedded in the brain, we don't have to think about lifting our foot eight inches up and forward; our brain simply directs our body to do it. In the same manner, our brain recognizes particular social situations and engages the appropriate neuro-network that directs the body to respond in a specific manner without conscious thought. As we move from childhood to adulthood, we rely increasingly on these automatic behaviors with their attached feelings and thoughts. These work on an unconscious level and become the basis of our personality, beliefs, and ways of perceiving the world.

BELIEF #4: WE HAVE THE NATURAL ABILITY TO CHANGE AND RE-CREATE OURSELVES.

Humans can change. Not only can we learn to act differently in the world, but we also have the ability to change the beliefs, attitudes, and patterns that form the foundation of our personal existence. This powerful belief contradicts the seemingly accepted notion that people do not or cannot change—"That's just the way she is" or "He's always been that way and will always be that way."

RELATED BELIEFS

Nothing needs to be wrong with a person in order for them to consciously desire to grow and change.

Wherever and whenever a person becomes inspired to change is the perfect time and place to begin that change.

Personal transformation requires conscious effort over time.

BELIEF #5: EACH OF US HAS A PATTERNED-SELF AND A ME-SELF.

Co-Counseling labels unconscious behaviors with their accompanying thoughts and feelings as *patterns*. Most people think of these automatic responses as "habit." In *The Power of Habit*, Charles Duhigg estimates that over 40% of everything we do as adults is done through habit—without conscious thought.[6] Co-Counseling draws a clear distinction between our operating unconsciously, calling this the Patterned-self, and our acting consciously, calling this the ME-self. The ME-self consciously created our patterns and can create alternatives to them.

There are two types of patterns: *chronic* and *intermittent.* *Chronic* patterns form the basis of our personalities. "He doesn't feel loveable." "She has no fear." They require long, conscious, sustained effort to change. *Intermittent* patterns have specific "triggers" that calls them forth. The key to creating alternatives to these *intermittent* patterns is to identify what triggers them. By becoming conscious of triggers, we allow the ME-self to create conscious alternatives to the pattern. In moving our lives forward, we need to understand the distinction between the Patterned-self and the ME-self while accepting and appreciating how they both serve us.

BELIEF #6: EACH OF US IS A UNIQUE INDIVIDUAL.

We may be remarkably the same in our physiological bodies, but each human contains a combination of nature and nurture resulting in an extraordinary distinctiveness among and between people. This distinctiveness is lost on many people, however, because they do not internalize (or make personal) the raw events of life. Each person has this ability; but because of the

107

constantly accelerating pace of modern life, people rush from one interaction to the next, from one meeting to the next, from one relationship to the next and do not take the time to internalize each of these events. By internalizing the raw events of life, we give personal meaning to them and through this process we begin to see our experience of the world as unique. If we do not give personal meaning to the events of life, we are destined to live on the surface of our individual world, where we begin to think of ourselves as the same as others. This opens the door to comparing ourselves with others—how I am the same or different from neighbors, coworkers, and friends. In doing this, we become dependent on comparisons for our personal worth and value. As people start to understand their experiences as unique, however, this type of comparison becomes meaningless. Co-Counseling holds that each person is unique and capable of developing a rich interior life that gives substance and meaning to ordinary, everyday experiences.

RELATED BELIEFS

We are the experts on our own lives.

We all know our lives better than any other person can know them. No anthropologist, guru, psychologist, sooth-sayer, or friend can know us better than we know ourselves. If we live only on the surface of our lives, it may seem like these people do know us. But as we internalize events and realize the depth of our self-knowledge, we begin to appreciate ourselves as the real experts on our own lives.

We have the answers to all our issues and challenges within ourselves.

We can read books, go to weekend workshops with brilliant thinkers, go to rehab centers, or pay a personal coach or therapist to assist us in the process of finding answers to our problems and concerns. Ultimately, however, we must determine for ourselves the answers to our problems and concerns. We make the final decision to take or refuse advice based on what we think, feel, and believe is right for us. To act solely on another's belief is to abdicate responsibility for our lives.

We alone are responsible for our thoughts, feelings, and actions.

109

We may not be able to control our exterior world, but how we react to it is our responsibility. Because something happens outside of us does not cause us to think, feel, or act in any particular way. The stimulus comes in and we process it internally; then we act or don't act. It is *our* choice. Co-Counseling accepts the model that thoughts cause feelings and that the combination of thought and feeling results in an action, the intensity of that action, or inaction. Blaming anyone or anything in the exterior world for how we think, feel, or act is a waste of time and a denial of our self- responsibility.

BELIEF #7: WE ALL STRUGGLE.

We all exist with our own personal issues and problems, joys and sorrows. We each have within us our own delicious, indescribable chaos through which we struggle to find our path. This grappling with life is unavoidable and can be considered simply part of the human condition. Our resistance to this natural phenomenon of struggle causes us to suffer—the more intense our resistance, the greater the suffering. As a person learns to have a reflective balance between his external and internal worlds, however, the resistance and, therefore, the suffering can cease.

Chapter 21

Sacred Space and the Use of Ritual

And a group—be it of two or fifty—
must have rituals to bind it together
and give it an identity.

—Chicago Tribune

Whether I am in the United States, Germany, Israel, or any other place where Co-Counseling is practiced, every training, gathering, or individual session begins with the creation of "sacred space." By sacred space I mean a space dedicated to the flowering of human potential, a space big enough to hold all of me: body, spirit, soul, mind. I want the space to be safe and comfortable with no trivial or demeaning conversations or comments. I want a space where I can connect to my inner self; space where I can be open and honest, cared for, and protected; space where I am respected for being me, and you for respected for being you.

Sacred Space And The Use Of Ritual

The idea of sacred space is not new. Churches, synagogues, and mosques are accepted as sacred spaces. They are places in which people find refuge from the fast pace of modern living. They are places where people can honor their inner world with its questions, issues, and beliefs. People go to cemeteries to honor both those who have died and their own emotional or psychological needs. Cemeteries give them this space and are, therefore, sacred. Native peoples have always held certain places as sacred: Stonehenge in England, Mt Katahdin in Maine, and Cape Reinga in New Zealand.

Co-Counseling does not own beautiful buildings or magnificent natural settings, so we always take the time to create sacred space through our intentional use of ritual. Whether it is two people meeting to do a session in an apartment, a small group meeting for a workshop or inquiry, or a large group at an international gathering, cocounselors transform their spaces from ordinary to sacred through the use of ritual. Ritual is a conscious act that can take any form as long as its purpose is to create the specialness or sacredness desired. In this consecrated space we want to be free to explore openly and honestly all aspects of our lives without fear of the judgments or evaluation of others.

In large and small groups the ritual happens in the opening circle. Each opening circle is different and reflects the intentions and desires of the particular group of people involved. Many opening circles begin with some form of physical movement ranging from dancing with music to stretching with conscious awareness of the breath. The purpose of the movement is to release some of the tension we carry in us as well as getting us in touch with our bodies and out of our heads. While moving, people often let out long sighs or other sounds that accompany the release of societal tensions. As the movement ends, a circle is formed and everyone joins hands. We close our eyes, take the time to feel our breath, and feel our feet on the earth (floor). At this point people may be invited to feel the energy in their own bodies, feel the energy of the people next to them, and then the energy of the whole circle. In this way individuals become grounded in both their own being and in the spirit and energy of the group.

We open our eyes and take time to look around, appreciating all the people who are part of the sacred circle we are creating. We may go around the circle sharing something of ourselves or do rounds with people validating themselves, and offering gratitudes or *new and goods* (See Chapter 30). The ritual can be simple or elaborate. The important fact is this happens each and every time we meet as a group for the purpose of Co-Counseling.

When two people meet to do a session, they decide what they need to do to create sacred space. It may not be a formal ritual like an opening circle, but they always take the time to transform the space they are in to a space appropriate for the purpose of cocounseling. They may simply silence the phone and put out the cat. They may place pillows on the floor and put out a box of tissues. They may simply hug each other or do some form of energy connection through "eye gazing" or "presencing" by which two people acknowledge the energy flowing between them. In Co-Counseling people are free to do whatever they need to do to create the space for their session, to consciously proclaim: "We are here to cocounsel."

Whether it is two people working in a session or a large gathering, once the opening ritual is completed, the people are bound together as cocounselors. These people, whether two or two hundred, become partners in maintaining the cultural norms and practices of Co-Counseling. Within this space they are peers, treat each other with complete respect, see each other as good to the core, and honor the sacredness of the human spirit within.

Just as there is an opening ritual at the beginning of each session or gathering, there is a closing ritual. At the end of a gathering, people come back together and form a circle holding hands. The closing ritual may mimic the opening ritual by having people close their eyes, focus on their breath, get grounded, and feel the connection with everyone else in the circle. The closing may be more elaborate and include movement, noise, or a song. Eye contact is often made among the participants celebrating connections as well as a fondness for each other. The circle normally ends with rounds in which people share what they got from the gathering and what they are taking with them. There can also be rounds of gratitudes and appreciations.

The closing ritual usually exhibits more intimacy and light-hearted energy than the opening circle because everyone has grown closer, having shared the experience of the workshop or gathering. When the formal ritual circle is complete, individual hugs are usually shared.

Sharing a hug of appreciation and caring seems to be the standard closing ritual for two people who have just finished a session. There is a celebratory feeling acknowledging the work they have done. They have been honest about their lives. They have revealed themselves in their full humanness with their fears, joys, problems, and successes. They may have cried, shook, pounded, danced, or sat and meditated. In ending their time together they simply feel more connected, more trusting, and soulful. Both the closing circle and the parting hug are rituals of transition. Cocounselors take the time to draw the session or gathering to an end by recognizing that they are leaving sacred space and entering the ordinary reality of the larger societal culture.

Chapter 22

Establishing a Sacred Relationship with Ourselves

The truth about my life:
I live a good life

. . .

a good life
and
my life can be hard

In any Co-Counseling event the opening ritual serves two distinct purposes. In the last chapter I focused on the use of ritual for the creation of sacred space. This is the collective responsibility of everyone present. They know once the space is established, the warm, accepting cultural norm of Co-Counseling emerges allowing them to step into its freedom and safety. In this chapter I examine the effect of the ritual on the individuals performing it.

117

Before an opening circle, participants often join together in physical movement. The activity can be as simple as swinging arms or stretching or as complex as yoga exercises. Many times the movements are accompanied by moans, groans, and sighs as individuals release the day's anxieties and stresses. The individuals involved determine the level of physical exertion. The intention behind the movement is to wake up the body.

Most of us take our bodies for granted. We spend most of our time sitting at jobs or in cars, watching television, or eating. When we do walk, we often ignore our bodies and focus instead on where we are going, who we are with, and what we are seeing while listening to music or talking on our smart phones. Thus in everyday life we lose connection to our bodies unless they complain. Starting Co-Counseling events with conscious movement helps ground us in our bodies and brings us into the present.

The physical exertion involved also releases the tension stored in our muscles. Daniel Goleman and Tara Bennett-Goleman state:

> "These muscle tension symptoms can be caused by emotional turmoil. Fear, anger and frustration register in the body's muscles, and the ones in the tension triangle [shoulders to the top of

the head] are quite sensitive to these emotions. Researchers have found, for example, that in the first two or three seconds of emotional upset, the muscles around the eyes, mouth and jaw almost always tighten."[7]

Relief from these tensions come through the stretching, gentle movement, and shaking exercises at the beginning of gatherings.

Co-Counseling is an in-the-body experience. We pay attention to the messages our bodies give us. These messages arrive as words in our heads, feelings in our guts, physical pains in our muscles, or passions from our hearts. The body plays a critical role in cocounseling practice, and the gentle movements and stretches involved at the beginning of the opening ritual serve to awaken the body and prepare it to assert itself.

While stretching, prancing, releasing muscle tension, and often laughing at ourselves, we build a sense of camaraderie with each other. Feelings of personal isolation usually vanish. A sense of being part of a whole gradually develops while we tune into our own bodies. We become more animated and engage each other while becoming more present for ourselves. As the activity ends and we gather in a circle, a relaxed quiet emerges from the exuberance of the physical activity.

Joining hands with the individuals on each side of us, we form a circle, close our eyes, and take the time to become conscious of our breathing. Usually we take several deep breaths and concentrate on the air flowing into and out of our bodies. We pay attention to our physical presence, from our feet planted firmly on the earth (floor) to our hands that are holding and being held by the hands of those next to us. We pause, taking the time to appreciate ourselves while feeling the energy flowing through our bodies. The pause here is important and can last for several breaths. During this time we come home to ourselves and feel our wholeness.

We open our eyes and look around, appreciating the people in the circle. We see both familiar faces and new faces. We are part of the circle, and regardless of why we are there each of us is an important part of the whole. Our individual energy, our presence in the circle, helps make the circle what it is. Without each person in it the circle would not be the same. By acknowledging the importance of the circle, we are acknowledging our own importance. In this way people in the circle become grounded in their own beings and in the spirit and energy of the whole.

When the silent acknowledgment of self and others is complete, we usually go around the circle sharing something of ourselves. This "check-in" is normally short and allows each of us to share something important we are carrying into the event. When the "check-in" is complete, rounds of validations, gratitudes and *new and goods* follow.

From the physical movement before the circle forms to the final offering of gratitudes, the ritual opening encourages a personal transformation within each participant. By simply being part of the circle, we physically remove ourselves from the immediate demands of day-to-day living. Having become fully present for ourselves, we become mentally and emotionally distant from those same demands. Not that the responsibility for children, parents, jobs, pets, plants, and personal safety disappear, but rather it is placed in abeyance within the sacredness and safety of the space created. During our time together we view and explore our lives without concern for the immediate and practical consequences of what we do or say.

In this space we take the time to honor ourselves. We don't have to worry about what anyone thinks. Here we are accepted as good to the core. Here we can explore all our relationships. Nothing needs to be hidden for fear of judgment. Here we gain perspective on various aspects of our lives without concern for how what we say or do will impact others. Here we slow down and get in touch with the feelings we often have to ignore just to get through the day or a meeting. Here we make the time to move beneath these feelings to examine the emotions energizing them and keeping them alive.

The transition into a sacred relationship with ourselves allows us to notice and respect the messages our bodies give us. Here a person stops relying on the brain and its rational thinking as the sole basis of decision making, which is emphasized and insisted upon in most homes and classrooms. As children many of us were taught to dismiss anything not logically connected to the task directly in front of us. In this way children are discouraged from taking their spontaneous thoughts seriously. These intuitive thoughts are often referred to as *random,* and children are told that these thoughts are unimportant and get in the way of clear thinking. "What has that got to do with what we are talking about?" is a familiar phrase from my childhood and from those of many people who come through my courses. Part of developing a sacred relationship with the self is accepting and appreciating the importance of intuition and gut instincts. In the space of a session or gathering, a person can take the time to uncover the basis of intuitive thoughts or explore the source of gut instincts.

Children are also taught not to let emotions get in the way of their thinking. Society's belief is that the basic emotions (sadness, fear, anger, and joy) get in the way of rational, relational thinking. Classroom teachers seldom tolerate the expression of emotion, which is viewed as disruptive. Students rarely can display their emotions. They are 'shushed' and reprimanded for being emotional. Daydreaming is discouraged as a waste of time. In my trainings I ask if anyone remembers positive messages about emotions from childhood. In most courses not even one person can recall anything about emotions being considered a positive asset.

In most of our schooling the rational, linear functioning of the brain is of primary importance and is the basis of how we are judged. Anything that interferes with it is dismissed as meaningless. In these ways, we are taught not to trust our instincts, whether they manifest themselves as intuitive thoughts, gut instincts, or feelings tied to emotions.

Yet as adults we know spontaneous thoughts and feelings continually happen; there is no stopping them. The biochemical-electrical brain-body we dwell in reacts automatically to internal and external realities whether we are aware of them or not. We are one whole, integrated computer operating over 99% of the time without conscious direction. Our wonderful brain-body does not spit out random thoughts or trivial feelings or purposeless emotions! When these events happen, something called them forth. They are meaningful, even if we do not know why they occurred. Based on early childhood training, however, we ignore and repress them. We treat these messages from the body as arbitrary and meaningless.

In Co-Counseling we honor our whole being as sacred. We learn to listen to the messages it gives us. We learn to pay attention to the tiniest feeling. We do not dismiss what the brain-body gives us. We learn over time to trust the messages we get and work with them. There is nothing arbitrary or meaningless about the emotions in the gut or the voices in our head or the gut instinct waiting to be recognized. In Co-Counseling we give the body the true dignity it deserves. To treat it any other way is to deny our real human self-worth. We are incredible beings on an amazing journey through time and space. Our bodies are more than just the physical vehicles carrying us on this journey; they are the source of our intuition and love. Not to treat them with the greatest respect is to deny ourselves the true beauty, wisdom, and inherent power of our brain-bodies.

Establishing a sacred relationship with ourselves is the key to the power and effectiveness of Co-Counseling. In the role of the self-counselor we tune into the messages from our gut and heart as well as the cranial brain. In this role we take the time to be aware of our history, the present, and the future. We explore current issues and heal historic wounds. We allow ourselves to dream and envision a life unfettered by past or present limitations.

ESTABLISHING A SACRED RELATIONSHIP WITH OURSELVES

We let our spirits soar while experiencing the depth and power of our emotions. We are free to feel light and heart centered, unburdened by the weight of practical reality. Here we transcend the ordinariness of daily existence and allow ourselves to see the sacred journey of life. And from this place of internal connection and reflection, we learn to accept and celebrate the life we are living.

Chapter 23

Session Partners

All the world is a stage
And all the men and women merely players;
Each has their exits and their entrances;
And one man in his time plays many roles.

—Shakespeare, *As You Like It*

You may start Co-Counseling because you have unresolved issues in your life or you are simply curious. For whatever reason you decide to take the Fundamentals training you discover immediately the basic work of Co-Counseling is done within the sacred space of a session. In this space you step outside of the chaos and challenges of ordinary life. Here you can relax. Here you have no history and no obligations to anyone other than yourself and your session partner. You don't have to please anyone. Session partners are allies in the work of Co-Counseling. The two of you form a dyad of trust and caring even if you have never met before. There is a sense of timelessness in these sessions where the only reality is what happens within the session.

The session is your stage, and on this stage you and your partner will play two complementary roles—The self-counselor and the co-counselor. During a session you will have the opportunity to ground yourself in each role. Session time is divided in half, so session partners have equal time in each role. While in the role of the co-counselor you witness, support, ground, and assist your partner, who is in the self-counselor role. This is basically done by providing caring-aware-attention and respecting the confidentiality of what is spoken. As the self-counselor you are in charge of what you do, how you do it, and what you take with you when your time in the role ends.

When you and another person choose to have a session, there is an unspoken agreement between the two of you that all Co-Counseling guidelines and practices will be honored. After deciding to have a session, the two of you determine how much time you want to spend in the session and where you want to hold it. Once this is settled, each of you gets whatever you might need to prepare the space for your time in the session: pillows, backjacks, tissues, paper, pens, and the like. After preparing the space, each of you takes the time to presence yourself both in your own being and with your partner. This simple exercise grounds the both of you while acknowledging your connection with each other. Then together the two of you decide who will be the self-counselor first. This decision is usually based on individual need or preference.

By the act of creating and entering sacred space, you and your session partner acknowledge your common humanity, peerness, and desire to bring clarity to your lives with the belief you are both good to the core. Being able to make these acknowledgments enables you to ground each other in present-time reality and provide the safety and support needed to enter internal realities that may be unknown. The power of the session is liberating because each of you is completely free to explore your life in front of the other. No one is judging or evaluating you. In the role of the co-counselor you validate the self-counselor's work by giving the gift of caring-aware-attention.

Although you and your session partner may be different in a billion ways, in terms of the basic human journey the two of you are remarkably the same. You were both created in the union of a man and a woman. You both spent many months in a watery womb before being born into the earth's environment. You were both raised by imperfect people, developed patterns as children that may no longer serve you, received some form of education, and learned to live in a world of relationships with all their corresponding joys and problems. Lastly, you are both growing older every day, and you are both going to die.

SESSION PARTNERS

Seeing each other as human, the two of you become remarkably the same regardless of race, ethnicity, gender, or economic circumstances. You may not even speak the same language, but each of you knows the other has gone through the Co-Counseling training and respect each other's commitment to conscious living and personal growth. Here your compassion can manifest itself, and empathy can flow between you. As humans you are of equal worth, and what you bring to the session is priceless—your humanity and human spirit.

Chapter 24

Self-Counselor Essentials: Self-direction and the Truth

The best mind-altering drug is truth.

—Lily Tomlin

For whatever reason you choose to participate in Co-Counseling, you find yourself actively exploring and examining your life in the role of the self-counselor. Here your time is unencumbered by any demands except what you put on yourself. Your session partner is there to support you as you uncover thoughts and emotions that may be hidden under facades of politeness and civility. In the training course you are taught many skills, techniques, and procedures to enhance your work of exploration. There are two essentials that cannot be taught, however,

SELF-COUNSELOR ESSENTIALS: SELF-DIRECTION AND THE TRUTH

and without which no meaningful exploration will happen. The first is learning to be self-directed, and the second is becoming deep-in-the-gut honest.

A unique feature of CCI Co-Counseling is that, when you are in role of the self-counselor, you are 100% in charge of what you do and how you do it. This sets it apart from other therapies or counseling practices in which a professional helps steer you through a session. In Co-Counseling, no one gives you suggestions, no one reminds you what you said in a previous session, no one tells you what you should do or not do, and no one steers you. You make all the decisions about what you do and how you do it. Lastly, you are solely responsible for what you get from your time in the role.*

During most of the fundamental training, the time you spend in the self-counselor role is structured specifically to give you the opportunity to learn the skills and techniques being taught. This is experiential learning. In these sessions you and your session partner use the skills and techniques immediately after they have been explained. In the sharing rounds that follow,

---

* All Co-Counseling communities are autonomous, and as such there are many names for the role of self-counselor: 'client', 'worker', 'explorer', and 'enquirer'. The role evolved from the concept of "the client" as it has been and still is used in the world of psychology, from which Co-Counseling emerged 50 years ago.

each person has the opportunity to ask questions or make comments on their experiences. It is my observation that the thoughts and concerns expressed in these rounds deepen the participants' understanding of the technique just practiced. It is another example of how Co-Counseling teaches us to learn from each others' experiences.

Near the end of the training there is unstructured session time is which you can do whatever you want while in the role of the self-counselor. The idea behind these open sessions is for you to start experiencing self-direction. During them you may run out of things to examine and end up sitting in silence. Running out of things to talk about could indicate you are examining only the surface reality of your life, you don't know what to say without the stimulus of a social conversation, or you have developed the habit of having a 'professional' give you direction. For whatever reason you simply run out of things to explore.

On the other hand some people can simply talk, talk, talk without thinking or feeling. This is another manifestation of living on the surface of existence. These people can talk for hours, telling stories about themselves and others while never discovering meaningful connections with their internal world.

Many people don't have any idea what it means to explore their internal life or are terrified to do so. It takes courage to look inside and be willing to examine and feel what you find. There might be conflicting thoughts, unpleasant memories, emotions, feelings, and voices questioning everything. Human beings are infinitely complex, and what dwells inside us can seem overwhelming. To a person beginning a journey of self-exploration, the internal world may seem like an unfathomable abyss. When you gaze into yourself, what may gaze back at you, whether you want to see it or not, are feelings and truths about your life.

Co-Counseling is not a social conversation. Your session partner, the co-counselor, supports and witnesses you and your work. Your partner is not there to guide you or fill in the silences. It is critically important that no one gives you suggestions about what to do next. If this happens, you may never become truly self-directed. You could easily become dependent on interventions from the co-counselor to do *your* self-exploration. This would take away the true power of Co-Counseling as self-therapy. You are your own healer. You are your own counselor. You are your own therapist. The techniques and skills taught in the Fundamentals training help you discover and explore your internal world and also help you emerge from your exploration with knowledge and insights about your life.

As you begin cocounseling you start opening the meta-
phoric doors to your internal life. Scary? Damn right!
Within the nourishing energy of the training and the safety of a session, however, you gradually move through your
fears and begin to be self-directed. At first, you might just
dip into the feelings you are having, noting what they are
and where they are in your body. Then you start search-
ing for the thoughts that trigger the feelings and what
emotions energize them. You might initiate working on
a major issue that has persisted in your life. As you exercise your newly acquired abilities in self-direction, you
learn that, whatever subject matter you immerse yourself
in you always emerge in the caring-aware-attention of the
co-counselor. Slowly it becomes easier for you to dive into
the abyss. Each time you dive, you become more comfortable with whatever doubts and fears you find. You begin exploring what lies behind and under your choices.
During these first forays into your interior world, you begin appreciating how empowering it is to be self-directed. This learning cannot be taught. It has to grow from
actual experience. As you direct your session work, you
develop an in-charge attitude leading to a total sense of
self-responsibility for all aspects of your own life.* This is

---

* This practice brings alive the serenity prayer used in Alcoholics
 Anonymous—

 'God grant me the serenity to accept the things I cannot
 change,
 The courage to change the things that I can,
 And the wisdom to know the difference."

all spoken in the Fundamentals training, but it needs to be learned, accepted, and embraced by you through actual practice. If you do not actively utilize self-direction, you will never realize the full potential of Co-Counseling.

There is nothing fancy about what you do in the role of the self-counselor. As you grow to accept your whole life as your responsibility, you begin to realize the importance of staying in touch with your interior world. This involves sorting through layers of stories with their truths, half-truths, and untruths, all created in the past and all serving as justification for living the life you are living. You may also have to confront where you are living 'in truth' and where 'out of truth' in your current day-to-day life.

Early in life young people can find out that being truthful does not always fit their plans or purposes. They may learn to avoid telling the truth because doing so could affect them or others negatively. The truth could get them sent to bed without dinner, kept after school, cost them a friendship or a place on a school team or play. As adults, the truth could get them fired, divorced, attacked, or left without a friend. So people constantly bury the truth, and by the time they begin examining their interior life, these truths are concealed under years of stories filled with little distortions and untruths that feel familiar and comfortable. Many times these individuals don't even know their own truths. They live in swamps of confusion

135

where they make up convenient stories to look good and be accepted. Yet every time these stories are spoken or even thought, their bodies tense and they feel something is not quite right. The body knows the truth; falsehoods never fool it. On the other hand, when people speak truth, their bodies relax and feel strong.[8]

In the safety of a session you might explore a personal situation causing you trouble. You may examine the relationships among the people involved, their histories, how the situation developed, where it might be heading, and your part in it. In this work you gain a perspective on the whole situation from the safety and timelessness of a session. You can decide where you stand in relation to the others involved and what you can do to settle your part in the situation. It can take real effort to sort through the confusing complexities involved in a situation before you discover the truth about where you stand and what you want. At other times a truth might emerge from under layers of stories and make-believe thinking the minute you shine the light of conscious inquiry on it. In discovering these truths about yourself, you begin to build equilibrium between your internal and external worlds. In finding, acknowledging, and accepting your truth, you may change relationships, jobs, and the direction of your life. Becoming confident of your truth is crucial to the work of self-discovery and personal growth.

136

Knowing you are being truthful can propel your life forward. When you finally identify and speak your truth, you become more spontaneous, open, and energetic. So the often-cited biblical quote from John, 8:32 "Then you will know the truth, and the truth will set you free," is real. Sadly, however, the admonition attributed to President James A. Garfield is also real: "The truth will set you free, but first it will make you miserable."[9] As you begin to speak and live your truth, your life changes, and living your truth can be surprising and upsetting to others. So as you let your truth be heard, your world changes. This may not be easy, but it is critical to living an honest life, and only in honesty do you and your relationships truly grow.

In the role of the self-counselor you learn to be self-directed and speak your truth. These are the keys that unlock your internal world and free you to live spontaneously in the moment. Sometimes realizing a truth may surprise or even startle you because it has been buried for so long. When truth emerges, you may refuse to acknowledge it because it will change your relationship with some part of the world. Being self-directed, however, you cannot ignore the truth. Every time you cocounsel, you are confronted by it. It demands to be known and acted upon. If the truth you have discovered is not what the world thinks your truth is, speaking it outside the safety of a cocounseling session may change your world. So you may choose to practice speaking it within a session and explore the feelings that come up in you as you say it. You may also want to examine the possible consequences of saying it outside the session. Inside the session, however, you can do what you need to do to prepare yourself to speak your truth so it will be heard and honored in the world.

Dealing with unspoken truths is great material for session work, and, like all session work, it prepares you to act strongly in the world. Learning to be self-directed in sessions helps you become self-directed in your life. Learning to speak truthfully in the world makes it easier and easier to accept yourself as good to the core. Consciously speaking the truth frees you to be fully engaged in the world. You may have to learn how to deliver your truth tactfully, but expressing your truth permits spontaneity and openness. Lastly, being truthful in your sessions and experiencing the freedom this brings you in the world encourage you to keep cocounseling on a regular basis.

Chapter 25

The Co-Counselor and the Meditative Mind

No man is free who cannot command
himself.

—Pythagoras

In the role of co-counselor you sit across from the self-counselor and serve as an anchor as they do their work. You sit quietly, witnessing everything he says and does. You are fully present as he pours out tears of sadness, speaks a truth he may have never spoken before, or releases pent-up frustrations. By simply being present for the self-counselor, the co-counselor validates the person's truth, pain, joy, hopes, and dreams. Why do we share our lives? We do it so another person knows what is going on with us—so we are not alone in our struggles. We do it so we do not drown in our own internal drama. The person listening completes the basic human need we all have to be heard, understood, and accepted.

When I teach Co-Counseling, I begin with the role of the co-counselor because it is the more difficult of the two roles to learn and its importance is often lost in the excitement generated in the role of the self-counselor. What people learn about themselves in the role, however, is as vital to their healing and growth as anything they learn as the self-counselor. The role completes the personal fulfillment a person experiences doing sessions. Becoming an excellent co-counselor is critical to becoming a practitioner of Co-Counseling.

When you begin a Fundamentals training, the role of the co-counselor is seldom understood for the importance it holds in the Co-Counseling process. You come to the training to work actively on your life, work that seems to occur solely in the role of the self-counselor. It appears that all you do as the co-counselor is sit and listen to the self-counselor. Although it may look that simple, the role of the co-counselor demands a self-discipline not easy to master. It requires practice and conscious effort to achieve the self-awareness necessary to become skillful in the role.

In England, Co-Counseling communities state the basic job of the co-counselor (whom they call the 'helper') is to be *out with* the self-counselor. Being *out with* the other person means there is no place for thinking while in the role of the co-counselor. As soon as you start thinking about anything, you are in you own head and not *out with* the other person. The task of the co-counselor is to witness and support the self-counselor. You are not there to fix the other person or to examine what he is sharing. The instant you do any of this, you are no longer fully *out with* the self-counselor. Your attention is now partially focused within your brain.

So the first essential skill you need to master in the role of the co-counselor is staying *out with* the self-counselor. Essentially this means you are not thinking. Your brain is not engaged. This requires incredible discipline. You have to pay complete attention to the self-counselor and hear what he is saying without getting distracted by what he says or does, events in the immediate environment, or matters in your own life. You have to learn to listen without mentally evaluating or judging what the person is saying, how he is saying it, or what he is doing physically. All of this requires learning to quiet the brain.

Most people find staying focused solely on the self-counselor without brain chatter extremely difficult. In the role of the co-counselor we learn to take a break from our normal role as the analyst of everything. To stay *out with* the self-counselor requires us to silence our

141

brain; however, the brain doesn't want to be silent—it wants to analyze, judge, and fix.

In our everyday lives we compare and contrast our thoughts on a subject with the thoughts expressed by a speaker. We learned this as children while listening to adults talk to each other and to us. In these conversations they continually modeled a pattern of judging and evaluating the content of people's statements. Parents always want to know what their children are doing and how we were doing it. Then they evaluate and judge heaping praise or criticism based on their evaluation. Thus, as children we acquired a pattern of judging, analyzing, and evaluating as an essential part of our listening skills and have adhered to this pattern ever since. The pattern is very strong because we continually reinforce it every time we listen to anyone speak.

After thirty, forty or even fifty years of fine-tuning this pattern of listening, you must disengage from the pattern when you step into the role of the co-counselor. In my classes people in the helping professions have the hardest time quieting their brains and staying *out with* the self-counselor. Not only do they have the childhood pattern of mental engagement, but they also have been professionally trained to be involved directly and actively with their 'clients' in situations having the appearance of a cocounseling session.

The Co-counselor And The Meditative Mind

Learning to be a good co-counselor is not easy. It takes time and patience to become comfortable being *out with* the self-counselor. Patterns are hard to escape. We cannot simply wipe out the neuro-network containing our automatic, unconscious pattern of listening. We need it in our everyday life. It doesn't serve us, however, in the role of the co-counselor; therefore, we consciously need to develop an alternative neuro-network in which the brain is quiet and still. This requires retraining the brain. We do this by staying conscious of being *out with* the self-counselor every time we assume the co-counselor role. It is only through repetitive practice and self-discipline that we can develop this alternative neuro-network and activate it when we sit in the co-counselor role.

In my courses I relate a story Jack Kornfield tells about learning meditation. I do this because learning to be *out with* the self-counselor is like meditating. Kornfield says training the brain to be still and meditate is like training a puppy to sit. You tell the puppy to sit, petting it and giving it lots of attention. As soon as you stop giving it attention, however, it may wander away, exploring the world as puppies will do. After a time, you walk over to the puppy, pick it up, and, speaking lovingly to it, bring it back to where you want it to sit. You don't raise your voice; you don't yell at the puppy; you simply put it back down and say strongly and affectionately, "*sit.*" This time the puppy might stay a little longer, but it will wander away again

143

and again. Each time it does you go find it, give it lots of love and caring, set it back down, and tell it to sit. You keep doing this till gradually the puppy learns to sit and stay seated when you tell it to sit.

This is what we must do to retrain our brains. As co-counselors we start sessions being *out with* self-counselors, but then our brains wander away, attracted by spontaneous thoughts. It may take time before we realize we are now in our heads and not *out with* the other person. When we become aware we have drifted into thinking, we gently and lovingly bring ourselves back to being *out with* the self-counselor. We keep repeating this cycle, becoming aware of our wandering brains a little bit quicker each time it strays. After a time we find ourselves staying *out with* the self-counselor for longer and longer periods of time without wandering. Each time we consciously stay *out with* the self-counselor, we are imbedding the new neuro-network in our brains. Once the network is in place, we can consciously and easily access being *out with* another person whether we are in a cocounseling activity or not.

I will say much more about the role of the co-counselor in Part Six. For now it is enough to say that learning to be a co-counselor is not easy. Being *out with* the self-counselor is akin to meditation. Both require a stillness of mind and a steady, open focus. In Co-Counseling, being *out with* the self-counselor means staying completely attentive to the

144

individual as he is working on his life. Because you hold him as good to the core and are clear of all judgments and analysis you can be the neutral ground, the human connection that anchors him in present reality. You, as the co-counselor, metaphorically (and sometimes in actuality) hold his hands as he creates and re-creates his life, deals with patterns that no longer serve him, and engages his emotions as positive allies. By being *out with* the self-counselor and, therefore, fully present for him, you are providing a wonderful gift that comes naturally from the human spirit and is felt by the human spirit of the self-counselor.

Part IV

An Introductory Gathering

Prologue

Co-Counseling does not have a one-model-fits-all dogmatic basis. In July, 1998, when Co-Counseling teachers representing communities in Europe and the United States gathered in the northern part of the Netherlands to discuss what they taught in their Fundamentals, they gathered as peers. The list they generated has served as a common base for all trainings since the meeting. Teachers would continue to focus on the elements they thought were most important while agreeing that all the basics from the list would be taught. They also agreed that what they taught would not be limited to the list. There were no discussions about *how* to teach any of the elements. The list is important because it guarantees that all cocounselors attending national and international workshops share the same basic knowledge and conception of the cocounseling process and the elements thereof.

The basic elements of Co-Counseling are taught in a Fundamentals training. The training is usually preceded by an introductory gathering, which gives people new to Co-Counseling the opportunity to learn the basics and do a short session. Within the United States the content of these is basically the same but the form varies from teacher to teacher reflecting their personal styles. These Intros give people the solid information they need to make a decision about taking the Fundamentals training.

Many experienced cocounselors attend these introductory gatherings to show support for the teacher and Co-Counseling itself and also to talk about their experiences and how they have benefitted from their practice. Their statements add depth and richness to the conversations that take place. Their enthusiasm creates a strong, positive energy that flows through the gathering.

What follows is a description of a typical introductory gathering based on my experience. Other teachers may do their introductions differently, but will cover the same basic material.

Chapter 26

Welcoming

Heaven have mercy on us all—Presbyterians
and Pagans alike—for we are all somehow
dreadfully cracked about the head and sadly
need mending.

—Herman Melville, *Moby Dick*

During an introductory gathering I hand out a single
sheet of paper entitled "The Basic-Basics." At the top of
the sheet is the above quote from the great American
novel *Moby Dick*. Written in 1851 before the days of modern psychology, these words of Melville's protagonist,
Ishmael, assert that none of us escapes unscathed from
the realities of living in an imperfect world. We have all
been twisted and shaped by the world in which we live.
Most people keep moving from day to day with *survival*
as their primary goal. Survival may mean physical survival, such as getting enough to eat and maintaining a
roof over your head; mental and emotional survival, such

as dealing with the constant stress and anxiety of modern living; or material survival, which involves paying the mortgage on a house or, in the extreme, maintaining the family yacht. People dealing with survival do not necessarily have the desire or time to examine consciously the *cracks about their heads* or to engage in *mending* their lives. Some people show up at an introductory gathering aware of exactly what the cracks are and want to mend them; others have a vague sense something is cracked and want to discover what it is; still others are simply curious about what goes on in their heads; and lastly, some come just to learn about Co-Counseling itself.

When you come to an introductory gathering, I want you to know you are not alone in your desire to mend your life. The quote from Melville simply demonstrates that people have been wanting and needing to do this for centuries. The fate of human beings seems to be that all of us are *cracked about the head* and have the desire to mend the cracks and, in the process, create a better life for ourselves. Karl Jung believed that all humans have a natural desire to move their lives toward wholeness. Abraham Maslow viewed humans as naturally moving toward what he terms "self-actualization."

A critical time in peoples' lives occurs when they recognize that their feelings, thoughts, and behaviors are causing problems that are not going away. They may not be clear about the source of the difficulty, but they can no longer pretend nothing is wrong. Thus in the very first paragraph of *Moby Dick*, the character, Ishmael, announces that

> Whenever I find myself growing grim about the mouth; whenever it is a damp, drizzly November in my soul; whenever I find myself involuntarily pausing before coffin warehouses, and bringing up the rear of every funeral I meet . . . then, I account it high time to get to sea as soon as I can.[10]

He is telling us explicitly why he needs to do something about his life and exactly what he is going to do. For most of us, the manifestation of the *cracks about the head* may not be as clear as Ishmael's; but as unclear as they may be, we recognize we must act. In today's world we might not be able to get "to sea" in the same way as Ishmael, but we go on cruises through the vastness of the oceans or get on planes and travel thousands of miles to places where many of the daily struggles appear to be left behind. But in most cases we jog, ride bicycles, or hike up every climbable hill to escape the immediacy of our problems. Sadly, others turn to alcohol, drugs, food, computer games, and the like, for these same reasons. Still others choose retreats, weekend workshops, vision quests, massage, meditation, yoga, and other practices to regain a sense of peace while they live with the pressures of modern life.

151

Lastly others engage the services of psychologists, therapists, or twenty-first century coaches to assist them in healing the *cracks about their heads.*

Many people seek Co-Counseling after they have been involved with any of these professional ways of dealing with the stresses and problems of life. So the first thing I do when you come to a Co-Counseling introduction is acknowledge your courage for simply walking through the door. Your motivation may be unclear, but you are following a conscious, although not necessarily understood, need to act. Showing up requires a commitment to the self and a belly full of courage. For most people showing up at an introductory gathering is entering the unknown. Whenever we enter the unknown, we become aware of our vulnerability and at the same time want to stay open to what is new and different.

The space you enter will not be special. It may be in an apartment or house, or the basement of a church. There is no big yoga room, scented meditation space, or beautiful waiting room. Ordinary looking people welcome you. A buzz of excitement and the energy of expectation fill the space. Everything is simple. No clues exist to the expansiveness of the world of Co-Counseling.

During an introductory gathering people new to Co-Counseling readily mix with experienced cocounselors who have come to support the trainer and share what Co-Counseling means to them. In my house we congregate in the living room and kitchen and then move to a room empty of furniture where I ask people to sit in a circle. I introduce myself and ask people to share their names, where they are from, and how they heard of Co-Counseling. I talk a bit about how Co-Counseling has affected my life and ask everyone to share what brought him or her to the evening. The two most-common responses are the desire to change some aspect of life and curiosity. I talk about the Co-Counseling culture and begin with the creation of sacred space and the idea of creating a sacred relationship with ourselves.

At this point I invite everyone to stand and join hands in an opening circle. I ask them to say their names and share a feeling they are feeling. When we have gone around the circle, I direct them to close their eyes, take several deep breaths, and get in touch with their bodies from the tip of their toes to the top of their heads. I tell them that Co-Counseling is an *in the body* experience and that, in the training, they will come to know and explore the thoughts, feelings, and emotions running in their bodies. I ask them to open their eyes and urge them to look around the circle to see the people who are here—"Don't be afraid to really look at each other." Then we go around the circle again, saying our names and offering something we appreciate about ourselves. When this round is complete, I note that, through these simple conscious acts, we have come together and claimed this space for our evening's work. We have transitioned from ordinary space to what I call sacred space. I then urge them once again to look openly at each other and appreciate the courage each person possesses for just being here. This time they really look at each other, and as they do the energy in the room increases and becomes more peaceful.

Chapter 27

The Basics

Divine inspiration
only happens when there is space
slow down

. . .

breathe

. . .

trust
trust
trust

After the opening circle I talk of our *peerness*—pointing out that the circle we are sitting in has no beginning and no end. We are all equal in the circle. Within these circles we have unconditional, positive regard for each other. There is no place for put-downs or sarcasm of others or ourselves. I talk about the critical importance of *confidentiality,* which means all personal sharing said within the circle stays in the circle. Nothing leaves except knowledge of yourself and the Co-Counseling process. Strict adherence to *confidentiality* provides the safety we need to speak openly about our truths. We cannot be afraid that what we say or do in the circle might come back to harm us in any way. *Confidentiality* is essential to Co-Counseling. And nothing is secret about Co-Counseling itself. People can take home the process, techniques, and any other information about Co-Counseling and share it with anyone.

I talk about the two roles in Co-Counseling and emphasize how they are complementary and of equal importance; one cannot exist without the other. We do our healing and growth in both roles. This is why it is called *Co*-Counseling, and *Co*-Counseling is philosophically and psychologically different from conventional one-way counseling or therapy. In Co-Counseling the two people involved in a session are peers in their humanity. Both were birthed from wombs of darkness, are destined to die, and in between are busy living their lives the best they can. Our peerness allows us to sit and support each other, witnessing each other's lives with empathetic understanding. In the self-counselor role you are totally in charge of what you do and how you do it. Although this freedom is liberating, it is also scary. I often emphasize that, in the self-counselor role, you learn to pay attention to your own words and, in so doing, start to appreciate your own wisdom. In Co-Counseling we believe we have all the answers to our questions and problems inside ourselves.

THE BASICS

The cocounseling session is at the heart of Co-Counseling. A session normally consists of two people who take on the roles of self-counselor and co-counselor. The partners decide who will be in the role of the self-counselor first, and halfway through a session the partners switch roles. The partners normally sit opposite and close to each other, but can also stand, lie down, or go for a walk. When a person first begins doing the work of exploring her life, the partners need to sit directly facing each other in order to experience fully the wonderful, supportive energy of a Co-Counseling session.

In introducing the co-counselor role, I talk about the concept of caring-aware-attention. I talk about the importance of *caring* for the person in the self-counselor role and the belief we are all good to the core. I discuss the importance of the co-counselor staying *aware* of everything the self-counselor does—paying *attention* to the actual words being spoken, the inflection and tone of the voice, and any body movements, especially repetitive ones. I explain the co-counselor is not analyzing, evaluating, or trying to fix the self-counselor. The co-counselor is *out with* the self-counselor, engaging their heart and gut while silencing her brain—not easy to do.

Caring-aware-attention is one of Co-Counseling's pillars. Not only is it used in sessions, but it is also used whenever we are in a sharing circle or simply doing rounds. We

157

follow certain guidelines: We don't interrupt each other. We don't "cross-talk." We listen with our heart, gut, and brain while giving the speaker the energy generated by truly focusing our *attention* on her. We treat each other with respect and do not indicate approval or disapproval of anything a person shares. We simply listen, knowing what people are sharing is about themselves and not about us.

During the gathering I repeat several times that we are the experts on our own lives and are unique. No one shares our exact view of the world. Thus when we speak, we deserve everyone's respect and attention. In Co-Counseling we learn to focus our attention on who is speaking. We all deserve each other's respect. None of us has a monopoly on wisdom. The trainer may possess extensive knowledge and experience about Co-Counseling, but we all bring our experiences, knowledge, and wisdom into the room and deserve to be listened to when we speak. So by listening to each other, we learn from each other.

Lots of questions and discussion fill an introductory evening. A new person may inquire about something, and one of the experienced cocounselors is as likely to answer as is the trainer. All practicing cocounselors enthusiastically share their own experiences, and their comments add energy and insight to the discussion. Their remarks makes clear that everyone's experience in Co-Counseling is unique.

At the beginning of the evening, when I am explaining about the importance of *confidentiality*, I also state that it doesn't apply when we are talking about the nature of Co-Counseling or the techniques, skills, and practices involved. There are no secrets handshakes or practices. Everything is out front. I tell everyone that if you want to go tell your friends about Co-Counseling, please do it. It is free information, and the more ways it gets spread, the better our world becomes.

Chapter 28

The Contract

Become fully conscious
Know the journey you are taking
Then sunshine . . . rain . . . the same

The self-counselor is totally self-directed. While in the role,
you are completely in charge of what you do and how you
do it, including making a contract with your session partner and telling him exactly what you want from him. This
allows him to support you exactly how you want to be supported. This is called *the contract*. The co-counselor either
agrees or renegotiates the contract. It is imperative that
the co-counselor be aware of what you want while you are
in role of the self-counselor; otherwise he may do something that deflects you from the work you want to do.

Saying What You Want

Having to state a contract requires thinking about what
you want from the co-counselor. This is part of the general

focus of Co-Counseling on self-responsibility. Both you and the co-counselor are self-responsible. The contract is between equals. Therefore, when you offer the contract, be prepared for it to be examined before it is accepted. There are basic expectations that all self-counselors have of their session partners, but each and every time you are in the self-counselor role you state exactly what you want. Doing this helps develop a habit of thinking about what you want from a situation and being willing to state it. In this way you are learning a new, useful pattern that will serve you in your practice of Co-Counseling and in your daily life.

The contract is another feature of Co-Counseling that makes it distinctly different from professional therapy or a social conversation. In the world of professional therapy, this would be the equivalent of having clients stating clearly what they want and don't want from the therapist. The therapist would then have to agree or renegotiate the contract offered, thereby changing the usual power differential inside his office world.

The contract used in most Co-Counseling communities around the world consists of basic items discussed below which all cocounselors understand. It is called the standard contract. This can be added to, modified, and changed by the self-counselor. You might want your session partner to take notes or give you a five minute warning before your time ends. You can tell him you might

161

get up and walk around and, if you do, you want him to get up and walk with you. You may ask him to play a drum or give you a massage. The list is endless, and you know every time you state what you want the person in the co-counselor role can say *no*. Your contract is a straightforward request to the co-counselor, and once he has agreed, your time in the self-counselor role can begin.

The standard contract in the United States includes the following:

Caring-aware-attention
Eye contact
Touch or no touch
Facial affect or no facial affect
Interventions and what type of interventions
(for advanced session work)

Caring-aware-attention

The co-counselor's basic job is to give caring-aware-attention to the self-counselor. Part of giving this attention involves looking at the self-counselor's eyes even if his eyes are closed. This is of critical importance. Probably all of us know how it feels when we are talking to someone and they are not looking at us. In our culture making eye contact is not the norm, but we each know how enlivened we feel when we have a person's full attention as manifested through his eyes while we talk.

Eye Contact

A problem can develop, however, if the co-counselor takes his job of looking at the self-counselor's eyes too seriously and begins to stare intensely. This type of intense looking can feel like an intrusion where the message is, "you will not avoid my attention." This can be nerve racking and may remind a person of being a child when a parent or a teacher insisted the child look at the adult. The adult did this to gain control of the child and get him to stop some behavior, the adult—the big person standing over the small person—wanted the child to cease. So intense staring is not what is meant by eye contact in Co-Counseling.

When I was teaching an introductory evening in Ojai, California, a woman had real issues with the eye contact she received during a session. The woman said she did not like being stared at while she was talking. It made her nervous. Before I could say anything, her husband said it was not staring, but "receptive gazing." I asked him what he meant. He explained that, in receptive gazing, there is softness. There is none of the intensity associated with the demanding look of staring. There is openness on the part of the person looking. It is an invitation to the other person to speak, knowing they are being heard, respected, and accepted.

I loved the term and have used it ever since. To me receptive gazing involves the co-counselor gazing with respect at the eyes of the self-counselor while opening a channel to receive the energetic force the self-counselor is generating while doing his work. I also like the term "soft eyes."

I tell this story, not just because of the wonderful concept of receptive gazing, but to explain that Co-Counseling, rather that being a hide-bound organization, is instead open to new ideas and new concepts. It is constantly inquiring into its own structure and process in the same way practitioners are constantly inquiring into their own lives. In this way a person who came one evening and never showed up again added to the body of concepts used to explain a basic Co-Counseling idea.

Lastly, an expression I heard in yoga says simply; "Where the eye goes, energy flows." When we sit opposite a self-counselor, we are giving him energy to do his work. When I sit in the co-counselor role, I consciously open my crown chakra, let in the energy of the universe, and direct it through my eyes to the self-counselor. Humans are energy beings, and in Co-Counseling sessions and gatherings we take the time to be aware of the energy flowing through a space. As co-counselors we direct energy through our eyes to the self-counselor, who can get to the place where he feels held by the energy.

Touch

Touching in Co-Counseling is for the purpose of grounding, nurturing, and support. As part of the standard contract, cocounselors state clearly whether they want touch and, if they do, what kind of touch they want. Cocounselors always honor each individual's preferences to be touched or not touched and are very careful to respect a person's boundaries about where and how to be touched. The self-counselor may want to hold hands or to be touched in some way. Or he may want to touch the co-counselor in some way. Personal boundaries are always honored. You, as the co-counselor, can agree to the touching or say "no;" if you say "no," you might add a reason. You may also feel awkward with the type of touch being requested. If touch is essential to the self-counselor and the co-counselor says he doesn't agree then the self-counselor may choose to find another person with whom to do his session or do the session in accordance with the other person's wishes. In Co-Counseling a person always has a right to say "no" to any request whether it is about touch or anything else.

Facial Affect

Another part of the standard contract is facial affect. This may seem like a strange concern. Facial expression, however, is a key part of all face-to-face communication; and in Co-Counseling the co-counselor ideally sits directly in front of the self-counselor. Therefore, what the co-counselor does with his face is an important source of feedback to the self-counselor. The question then becomes, do you want instant feedback as you process your life? Do you want the approval or disapproval of the person sitting across from you? The general answer in Co-Counseling is "no, I don't want you judging my life. I don't want your feedback." Facial affect for many people, however, is an unconscious act learned in childhood. I learned to watch the faces of my mother, father, nuns, and all adults for their approval and disapproval. I, in turn, learned to give my approval and disapproval through my facial expression. I am not talking here of a smile or a frown, I am talking about a look of approval or disapproval. I am not sure what combinations of muscles in my face need to be contracted or relaxed to create these expressions, but the expressions nevertheless pop up on my face. In the co-counselor role I have to learn to control these judging faces so that I am not letting my face speak for some unconscious part of my being. Nodding the head is another way of indicating approval and disapproval and needs to be controlled.

In the co-counselor role, therefore, we learn to control at least some of our facial muscles, thereby minimizing the more obvious signs of approval and disapproval. We can control conspicuous smiles and expressions of sadness. Sitting directly in front of self-counselor, however, I develop a natural empathy to his shifting emotional reality. With my brain quiet, my gut and heart respond to what is heard in an untaught manner almost impossible to control. What is called the 'Duchenne smile' seems to be an authentic response to the joy of others and probably illuminates my face as I witness joy being expressed by the self-counselor. In the same unconscious manner, my face probably expresses sadness and anxiety as a natural response to the sadness and anxiety I observe in a self-counselor as he honestly examines his life. I may be fully out with person, but my response to his emotional reality comes from my gut and heart and shows up on my face.

So in Co-Counseling we learn to become aware of our face and what it is doing. If a self-counselor specifies he doesn't want facial affect, we can do it. On a deeper level, however, it is important that I express what is in me as a reflection of what is happening in the self-counselor. Carl Rogers, the father of client-centered therapy, states: "It is only by providing the genuine reality which is in me, that the other person can successfully seek for the reality in him."[11] This can be very subtle. We have to learn to trust ourselves, and our natural reactions, so that we are following, not leading, the self-counselor. I encourage new cocounselors to ask for 'no facial affect' when they are setting their contracts at the beginning of a session. In this way they get to experience how different "no facial affect" is from normal affect. I also suggest practicing no facial affect whenever they are in the role of the co-counselor.

Interventions

The last part of the standard contract is interventions. When people are first learning to be self-counselors, they are learning to be self-directed. They are learning to turn inward for answers rather than outward, which is the norm in our society. New cocounselors have to keep practicing being self-directed until they develop a new neuro-network in their brains that they can rely upon and trust. They have to develop the instinct to look inside for the answers to their concerns and problems. If people learning the role of self-counselor are given interventions when they are first learning to be self-directed, they will never develop the pattern of self-direction. They will become dependent on interventions to do their work, which is contrary to the principle of self-direction and, ultimately, self-responsibility. So interventions are introduced in the second half of the Fundamentals training and not before. I suggest to new cocounselors they ask for "no interventions" when they are setting their contracts.

Chapter 29

Sharing Circles

Unity of spirit
The earth . . . universe . . . all of us
What a grand mixing bowl!

When I finish going over all aspects of the contract, I ask
people to pair up to do a session. Once they are in pairs, I
have them choose who will be the self-counselor first and
invite this person to set a contract with the co-counselor.
I instruct the self-counselors to say, *"I want your . . ."* and
then have them go through the items in the contract that
we have just discussed. I explain to the co-counselors that
they should accept the contract as presented or state they
need to renegotiate it. I then tell the self-counselors they
have five minutes and encourage them to speak about
how they feel setting the contract. What is it like to tell
someone exactly what you want from her? Is this a new
experience or one you are used to? Do you see places in
your life where you might do this? I start the timer, and
the room comes alive with voices. They switch roles after

the five minutes; the new self-counselor sets her contract, which is agreed to or negotiated; then she has her five minutes to explore the act of saying exactly what she wants from another person.

Reflecting on your Experience

When the session is finished, everyone gathers into a circle and I ask them to share their experiences. After a short silence, someone begins, and then all participants get a chance to share what went on for them during the exercise and to ask questions. They cannot comment directly on what other people shared. They can say the same thing, but they have to own what they say and not refer to another person's experience. They have the right to pass if they have nothing to share or don't want to share. If they do, they simply say, "pass." When everyone else is finished sharing, they are given another opportunity to share. If they choose to pass again, the round is finished.

These rounds are called *sharing circles* and happen every time we finish a paired session or an exercise. In these circles each person gets the opportunity to share their personal experience of what they encountered during their time as the self-counselor. They can also comment on their time in the role of the co-counselor. They can ask questions, and if they do the trainer will normally answer, but others may join in and share their thoughts.

SHARING CIRCLES

Being open to everyone's thoughts reflects the Co-Counseling belief *we are all peer in our humanness.* Each person's thoughts reflect her unique perspective on any matter being discussed and, therefore, represent a viewpoint no one else can express. Sometimes a person in a sharing circle may say something in a way that makes clear a thought everyone else had been stumbling over. The trainer will have years of knowledge about the Co-Counseling process, but he or she is not the expert on the art of being in the world. In my trainings I always say: "If you look only at me for knowledge and wisdom, you are missing out on the knowledge and wisdom of the ten other people in our circle. Everyone is a teacher. No one has a monopoly on wisdom or the experience of living." In Co-Counseling we continually learn from each other.

After each exercise the sharing circle provides the opportunity to give voice to what you have experienced without fear of being judged or evaluated. As you share, each person in the circle gives you the same caring-aware-attention a co-counselor gives to a self-counselor during a session. The sharing circles give you the forum to speak honestly and be heard. In these circles you get to be heard, understood, and accepted for exactly who you are. I often think a major benefit of Co-Counseling is learning to express yourself fully and competently. An expression often used in Co-Counseling circles is to speak "*loudly and proudly.*"

When the sharing circle is finished, a buzz fills the room as people feel the sense of self-exploration engendered in the Co-Counseling process. The experiential part of the evening has begun.

Chapter 30

Appreciating the Self

Almost all of us enter adulthood afflicted with certain negative bias. We share a common tendency to blame ourselves, to see ourselves as bad, wrong, or in some way defective. It's as though we all, more or less, suffer from the same chronic "virus" of self-doubt.

—Leon F. Seltzer, *Evolution of the Self*

Some people arrive at an Introductory Gathering without a strong positive sense of self. They are filled with complex patterns of negative judgments and self-doubt, the lasting effects of critical parents and an educational system built on humiliation for motivation. These patterns acquired during childhood are re-enforced by society's negative bias, leaving many people insecure and unable to hold positive thoughts or images of themselves. People who want to change their lives need to grow beyond the negative default thinking that locks them into weak self-images.

To engage our interior life effectively, we must develop a strong, resilient sense of self. Without this, we will not acquire the self-acceptance needed to look inside without fear of what we will find. One of the most effective skills people learn when they first come to Co-Counseling is the art of validation. It is simple, easy to understand, yet challenging to put into practice. Once the skill is honed within the safety of Co-Counseling, validations can be brought directly into a person's daily life. They are a game-changer.

I introduce *validations* by explaining they consist of your name and a positive quality. I model the form: "I am Fred, and I am vibrant." "I am Fred, and I am studious." "I am Fred, and I am fun." We then go around the circle, and each person states his name and a positive quality. Most people find this exercise difficult after only a few rounds because they are not used to saying good things about themselves. Each person seems to have two or three qualities they can easily claim, but then find claiming other qualities more difficult.

A *VALIDATION*: YOUR NAME AND
A POSITIVE QUALITY

Invariably during these rounds, people use modifiers to limit or constrain the quality they are claiming, thereby making it easier for them to own the validation. I take this opportunity to emphasize that, if they can find the quality somewhere inside them, it is theirs—fully and completely. They own it. By claiming the whole quality, you are challenging the doubts and negative judgments you have about yourself. This is what Co-Counseling is about. If there are voices in your head yelling at you for claiming the quality, take the quality and the voices into a session and find out about the voices and why they are saying whatever they are saying. By claiming a quality and dealing with the voices attempting to rob you of it, you are beginning the process of self-analysis and growth. There is also no room in validations for comparisons or judgments, thus we never use the word "very," which invites comparisons and judgments.

If in Co-Counseling you can hesitatingly squeak out a validation, it is yours. It may feel strange at first to associate yourself with the quality, but after the tenth or twentieth time you repeat the validation, you begin to accept the quality as yours.

I talk about the importance of saying your name each and every time you give yourself a validation. By saying your name, you encourage your brain to identify the validation with you. You identify with your name. If someone shouts your name in a crowd, you turn around because there is a deep connection between you and your name.

175

By saying; "I am _____, and I am strong," you are being bold and declaring, "This is me, and I am strong." You
are making the statement to yourself and to the world.

After discussing modifiers and the importance of stating
your name when speaking a validation, I ask people to
pair up and do a session giving themselves validations.
The session is usually one and one-half minutes each way,
meaning each person will be in the self-counselor role
for that time. I tell them they can repeat validations, say
them loudly or softly, speak ones they hear other people
say, or be silent.

In the sharing round after the session, many people talk
about how difficult it was for them to give themselves
validations. I explain it is not surprising because most
of our lives we have been taught not to praise ourselves
or say good things about ourselves. If we praised ourselves as children, adults might giggle a little and say
how cute it is to hear Johnny or Mary say such a thing.
We might also hear, "Who do you think you are?" or "My,
you think a lot of yourself." As adults we might not hear
those words, but we can imagine them being thought.
Our peers, whether as a child or adult, might consider
us egotistical, vain, or boastful to praise ourselves. When
we are children, the teacher puts the gold star on our papers; we don't. Our parents say good words about us; we
don't. As young people we understood that we were not

176

to praise ourselves, and this became a pattern extending into adulthood.

When a child first does something that meets an adult's approval, he or she is probably praised when it happens. In a short period of time, however, this becomes expected behavior and the praise ends. Now, if the child falters, negative comments erupt from well-meaning adult. In general, when a young person makes a mistake, the adult using negative adjectives corrects him. The adults want the child to learn from his mistakes, so they cast the event in negative terms so the young person won't forget the mistake. Meanwhile, these situations imbed negativity into the child's consciousness. Children are deeply scarred by the negatives they are subjected to as they are growing up. Many of these negative comments stay with the child into adulthood, where they become negative default thoughts, which persist even when the person knows they are not true. I tell the story that my mother continually called me lazy, even though I am anything but lazy. Nevertheless, many times when I have slowed down and taken a rest, a little voice has jumped into my head accusing me of being lazy.

Validations are virtually miracle pills to confront negative self-judgment. In Co-Counseling we establish a *culture of validation,* meaning we don't put down others or ourselves. We don't use sarcasm or ridicule. We don't make disparaging remarks about each other. The *culture of validation* is insistently positive. By creating and maintaining this culture, people feel safe to try new things. If they make a mistake or if what they tried doesn't work, someone may note what has happened and encourage the person to try something different without casting negative judgments on the person. The culture of validation allows people to grow in a friendly, supportive environment without fear of being made wrong or bad.

There is a wonderful Youtube video about a parking lot attendant who validates his customers and, in doing so, brings joy to their lives and a smile to their faces demonstrating the power of validations. His validations are more elaborate than the ones we use in Co-Counseling, but they are equally effective. The short has been a Youtube hit since 2008, demonstrating how people love the concept and love to be validated.[12]

Another practice used in Co-Counseling to engage and expand a person's positive sense of self is called *New and Goods*. This exercise, rather than looking into our interior world to recognize positive qualities, looks at our exterior world to find, recognize, and bring to consciousness anything and everything good in our lives. Just like validations, the idea is simple, easy to understand, but challenging to use.

A New and Good is simply your name, the statement "my new and good is," and something new and good in your life. I model the technique: "I'm Fred, and my new and good is the beautiful day," "I'm Fred, and my new and good is a telephone call," "I'm Fred, and my new and good is my grandson." I emphasize new and goods can be big: I bought a house; or small, I found a dime. No one has to know the significance your new and good has for you, so you don't have to explain what you are claiming as a new and good. So new and goods should be kept short. You don't need lots of words to claim your new and good. In fact, using lots of words might wind your new and good into an old and bad. "I'm Fred, and my new and good is I got my car fixed and it rides good, but it was expensive." It is so easy for us to slip into being negative in our culture, which is bathed in negative thinking. So in using New and Goods we are bringing the good in our external world into our internal world, into our consciousness.

New and Goods are simply your name and the statement—"*my New and Good is*"—Then add your *New and Good.*"

Lastly I stress the importance of keeping the New and Good in the present tense even if it happened in the past. "I'm Fred and my new and good is the sunset last night." I then repeat it using the past tense so people can clearly understand the difference: "I'm Fred and my new and good was the sunset last night." I ask if they heard how using the past tense separates me from the event. We use the present tense because it is in the present tense that our body feels. We engage our world in the present moment, not in the past. Events from the past can affect us, but we have to bring them into present reality to do so.

We do a couple of rounds of new and goods and then share our experiences. People talk about how reviewing their lives for new and good things is different from what they normally do, and speaking about them is strange. Normal conversation is laced with the negative or troublesome aspects of their life, not the new and goods. They also note sharing positives from their world feels enlivening and positive.

We pair up, and each pair splits a three-minute session naming new and goods. I tell people it is all right to repeat the same one, and I encourage them to keep digging to find different events or happenings they can claim as new and good. We break up into dyads, and the person in the self-counselor role begins combing through his life for new and goods. After both people have had time in the two roles, we gather together into a sharing circle. People find that after they get started, new and goods roll out easier than validations. After the sharing I ask people how they are feeling, and the sense of well being expressed brings out grins and smiles as people look at each other. I point out the elevated energy in the room and people nod in agreement.

In doing New and Goods we are not only making ourselves aware of the many, many good things in our daily lives that we normally do not pay attention to, but we are also enabling our bodies to re-experience the good feelings within us that we originally felt when these events happened. New and Goods are mood changers. They bring people into the present moment to sense the positive aspects of life while, at the same time, they silence the "old and bads" with their associated stresses. People generally feel good when sharing the good things in their lives.

New and Goods and validations focus attention on positive aspects of our lives. Together they establish a spiral of self-worth that simultaneously encourages people to shed weak images of themselves and negative images of their world. By doing validations, we reach inside and discover qualities that have sustained us but are seldom acknowledged. At the same time we recognize new and good things existing in our external lives that also are infrequently acknowledged. Linking together these positive aspects of our internal and external lives create a spiral of positive self-worth. "I'm Fred, and I am thoughtful." "I'm Fred, and my new and good is sending a birthday card to my uncle." As one assertion starts reinforcing another, spiraling takes on its own power. "I'm Fred and my new and good is, I was on time for my appointment" might be followed by "I'm Fred, and I am organized." The New and Good stimulates the recognition of a positive quality that I then affirm within myself.

We speak these validations and New and Goods out loud, using our name, so that our brain hears the messages and directly associates them with us. We take all of this in as new information from the exterior world. We suddenly start hearing we are "powerful," "beautiful," "smart," and "delightful." Haven't we always wanted to hear ourselves being identified with these wonderful, positive qualities? At the same time we are doing validations we are noticing and appreciating the new and good things happening in our lives—"I ate well today" or, "My boss praised my idea" or, "My car ran well today." They are like a sword that cuts through the general negativity of our world. As we speak all of this out loud we begin claiming a greater, more resilient, potent, and more positive self. This positive sense of self begins to spiral, allowing us to see our good qualities and the new and good things in our lives. Wedded together, these practices create a dynamo of positive energy within us. This energy facilitates self-appreciation that leads to self-acceptance, which is the true base from which we can heal our past and create a future we love.

Engaging the world with these two practices is transformational, and I tell everyone in introductory gatherings that, even if they never take the Fundamentals training, they will start to move their lives in a positive direction simply by making use of these two marvelous ways to celebrate themselves and their life.

In the book *Tuesdays with Morey*, Morey, who is living with a terminal illness says, "Well, for one thing, the culture we have does not make people feel good about themselves. We're teaching the wrong things. And you have to be strong enough to say if the culture doesn't work, don't buy it, Create your own."[13] Co-Counseling has created its own culture, and the spiraling affects of validations and new and goods are part of that culture. Through these easy-to-understand practices, people start undoing the negative impact of the larger culture. Over time, claiming the positive qualities within us, and positives things in our world lead to a positive optimistic attitude that helps to create a positive world to live in.

Chapter 31

A Warning and a Break

May the sun warm your heart
May the moon warm your earth soul
May others love you true

I announce we will be taking a fifteen-minute break, but before we actually break I talk about the reality that Co-Counseling is not appropriate for everyone. John Heron says in his book *Helping the Client* that

> "[Co-Counseling] is not for those who are too emotionally distressed to give attention to a fellow human on a reciprocal basis. It is a tool for living for those who are already managing their lives acceptably by conventional standards, but wish significantly to enhance their sense of personal identity and personal effectiveness."[14]

In order to be a cocounselor, a person must be able to stay *out with* the self-counselor while in the role of the co-counselor and be able to keep confidentiality. Some people find doing one or both of these very challenging. Being able to stay out with the self-counselor requires a person to quiet her brain and in that silence maintain a distance between herself and the work of the self-counselor. Some people cannot do this and are repeatedly drawn into a person's work, ending up in their own heads either thinking about what the self-counselor is saying or thinking about their own work. They get swamped in their own internal process and are no longer out with the self-counselor. They lose their focus and in losing their focus they lose the ability to give the free attention the self-counselor expects and deserves. Since being able to stay out with the self-counselor is an essential part of Co-Counseling, a person who cannot do this cannot be a cocounselor.

The second reason a person cannot be a cocounselor is if she cannot keep confidentiality. You cannot talk about the content of a person's session or what happens in a sharing circle. Even the slightest hint that you cannot maintain confidentiality will keep any person in the self-counselor role from feeling safe. Safety here means the self-counselor absolutely trusts that everything she says or does in a session will stay in the session. Everything in a session and in sharing circles is 100% confidential. No Exceptions. So if a person cannot keep confidentiality, she cannot be a cocounselor.

Some conversation may happen around these ideas, but people seem to understand intuitively the necessity for these boundaries.

At this point we take the fifteen-minute break. The last thing I do before the break is remind people about confidentiality. I note we are all human, we are just learning about confidentiality, and we might slip. If someone does refer to something from a session or a sharing round, gently remind the person that what she just said is confidential. If everyone takes responsibility to maintain the culture, then no one has to protect the culture. There are no enforcers in Co-Counseling.

With that said, we take the break.

Chapter 32

Experiencing a Co-Counseling Session

Time . . . Compassion . . . Touching
Honesty in dreams and visions
Bring heart-felt humbleness

Once everyone is back in the circle, I ask for questions. The nature and type of questions or comments tell me what the group has absorbed and what remains simply "surface" information. This is also one of the many times I am grateful for experienced cocounselors being present. They answer many of the questions, expanding and deepening ideas presented in the first half of the evening. Whenever I do respond, they do not hesitate to add their thoughts and experiences, demonstrating there is no single "right" view on most matters in Co-Counseling.

When the questions subside, I introduce *What's on Top,* a technique used at the beginning of a person's time in the role of the self-counselor to clear out the many thoughts and feelings buzzing about inside him. You begin your work by giving voice to the specifics of these buzzings as they drone on within you, thereby letting them go. What's on Top vacuums up the debris of daily living so that we have a clean slate to work with during our session.

WHAT'S ON TOP—*what's buzzing inside you?*

What just happened? What's about to happen? What recent disappointments are you still carrying? What decisions have to be made? What worries and responsibilities don't let go? What feelings are attached to these *buzzings?*

Sometimes when doing What's on Top, however, a thought or feeling might jump out and demand attention *right now.* The realization that the matter is bigger than initially imagined happens spontaneously; and your body, knowing you are within the safe container of a session, directs you to work on the matter *now.* Whatever the matter is, it becomes your work and all of a sudden you are fully involved in your work. In Co-Counseling we say you have gone from What's on Top to *What's on the Bottom.*

Trust in this type of spontaneous "knowing" is one benefit of establishing a sacred relationship with ourselves.

You may have entered the session with a particular subject you were going to pursue, but something inside you says, "*Work on this,*" and you follow the knowing. You may have no idea where this new matter will take you or what you might uncover along the way, but you are willing to move in the new direction. In talking about this spontaneous process of knowing, I talk about Alice, in Alice in Wonderland, going down the rabbit hole. She doesn't know where she is going or even where she is. What she knows is she needs to keep moving, and this is what you do as the self-counselor when you begin a session. No matter where you start, you keep moving, being alert to every thought and feeling emerging within you. If you entered your time as the self-counselor with a compelling matter to work on but you drop into another piece of work during What's on Top, you could suddenly find yourself looking at the compelling matter from a completely different perspective. The new perspective may contain an insight that helps you clarify the matter, as happens to Alice in the 2010 version of journey into Wonderland.

In Co-Counseling you need to be in the present to do your work, and doing What's on Top brings you firmly into the present moment. You can't be helplessly caught in the past or future or distracted by some fantasy. Only in the present moment can you feel and experience your life. This is why so many self-help books talk about the

"Power of Now." In Co-Counseling we need to be in the *now* to do our work in both roles—the self-counselor and the co-counselor.

When I finish talking about What's on Top, I say we will be doing a session, but before we proceed I introduce an attention-switching technique called *Present Time*. We use the technique to ensure that the person just finishing his work in the self-counselor role is fully back in present-time reality before moving on to whatever is next. Present Time becomes a routine part of all Co-Counseling sessions. Sometimes, but especially when a self-counselor has done a piece of intense work, he may need time and space to transition back into present reality.

Here is another example of Co-Counseling culture honoring our humanness. Many times in daily life we are expected simply to switch from one thing to the next without being completely finished with what we were doing. Our fast-paced world does not honor transitions. A person just had a hard day at work and goes into the parking lot and can't find his car because he is pre-occupied with what just happened in the office. As he looks for the car he falls victim to the frustration that has been building all day. When he finally locates his car, he gets in, leans back in his seat, lets out a big sigh, and just sits and breathes and maybe listens to some music. If he starts to drive immediately, he will be finding fault with other drivers and his frustration will keep building.

Co-Counseling honors the transition from the work a person does as self-counselor to whatever is coming next through the use of Present Time. When a person finishes his work in the self-counselor role, the co-counselor will ask if he wants Present Time. If the self-counselor says "yes" or the co-counselor sees that he does in fact need Present Time, the co-counselor will ask a series of easy-to-answer questions or have the person get up and move about the room touching or describing things. There are almost an infinite number of ways to assist a person coming back after his time in the role of self-counselor. The co-counselor continues to ask questions or give directions until it is clear the other person is fully present.

Examples of Present Time techniques
To be used when the self-counselor finishes
working:

four red (green, blue, etc.) things
you see in the room
five things you see when you look out the window
four states beginning with the letter 'M'
Spell your name backwards

After providing some examples, I ask people to think up a Present Time and we go around the circle with each person offering an idea. Almost always I see someone wince as we go around. When we are finish, I note that some people may have problems with specific Present Times. Some people are not good in geography or math or might be color blind, so a Present Time involving any of these can cause distress. The person simply needs to ignore what has been said and ask for a different Present Time. I also strongly emphasize that the co-counselor should not go near the subjects the self-counselor was working on in his session. Doing so might put the self-counselor back into his work, which is the opposite of the purpose of giving Present Time. Thus don't ask a question about food if the person was just working on food issues.

Once everyone seems to understand the concept of Present Time, I invite them to pair up for a ten-minute each-way session beginning with What's on Top. After they have paired up, they choose who will be the self-counselor first. Then the people in the self-counselor role set the standard contract, and the people in the co-counselor role agree or declare their desire to rene-gotiate. I remind them about speaking truth no mat-ter how uncomfortable doing this might feel. I also remind them to pay attention to what is happening in their bodies. Lastly I strongly suggest the people in the co-counselor role focus on their breath as they give Caring-aware-attention.

After setting contracts, pairs begin; and soon a whirring energy fills the room. Self-counselors jump into exploring the ideas and feelings buzzing in them. When the timer signals the end of the ten minutes, most self-counselors are fully engaged in processing whatever they were processing. I remind each co-counselor to offer the person finishing his work a Present Time or two, and while they do this, the energy in the room comes to rest

The session partners switch roles, and the person now in the self-counselor role sets a contract, which is agreed to by the co-counselor, and the new self-counselor sets off exploring What's on Top. The energy level in the room rises once again.

When the session ends, people gather back into a circle and a sharing round begins. As in all sharing rounds everyone gets the time to talk about his experience in each of the roles. Invariably people spend most of their time talking about what they did in the role of the self-counselor. Generally people talk about how good they feel, having permission to go through the layers of what's on top. Some people express amazement at how different and special they felt having someone watch and listen to them with such caring attention. Most people are surprised at how fast the ten minutes went by, commenting they could have easily used twice as much time. We often go around the circle several times as people share their thoughts about what has been presented and what they have learned. Questions that popped up during their session are asked and answered. After two and one-half hours the excitement in the room is palpable as we finish the sharing round.

Chapter 33

Ending and an Invitation

So this long day ends now
My mind opens so that I may see
What joy I have in me

No two introductory gatherings are ever the same because
the people attending are never the same. Co-Counseling
does not contain a magic formula to be distributed in
a one-size-fits-all package. Co-Counseling is experiential,
and because of this an evening or a training will move at
a pace and direction appropriate to the people present.
Basic material will always be covered, but how it is covered is based on the interaction of the trainer (s) and the
people present.

I have grown to like the term that Richard Mills, a Co-
Counseling trainer in Leeds, England, uses to describe
his introductory evenings. He calls them "tasters." By

going over the culture, basic beliefs, the roles involved, a few practical exercises, and a free session, people get to savor some of the possibilities of Co-Counseling. The simplicity and power of the evening create an awareness of the potential nourishment the full Fundamentals training holds. To sit down with a friend and talk about your life is wonderful, but to sit and talk about your life within the open supportive framework of a Co-Counseling session allows a freedom we seldom get, even with the best of friends. In the confidentiality of a session, we can let our emotions surface and express them without being condemned. We can open the door into the mysteries of our lives without any fear of impacting our relationship with our listeners. We can say what we need to say without being positively or negatively judged by the co-counselor. We are truly free to explore our lives.

There is enough information presented in the introductory evening for a person to evaluate rationally the concepts underlying Co-Counseling. The ten-minute session and the mini-sessions centered on Validations and New and Goods give people a real sample of the basic process. Each person now possesses a realistic idea and a feeling for a session as well as a sense of the supportive energy generated in a Co-Counseling gathering. Given this knowledge I invite people to make a decision about taking the full Fundamentals training. I pass out index cards and ask people to write their names and contact information, indicate whether or not they plan on taking the training, and add any comments they want to make.

When I have collected the index cards I talk about an article written by John Talbot, an English trainer and thoughtful writer on the subject of Co-Counseling. He says a person needs to be self-empowered and have the ability to be self-directed in order to get the full benefits of what Co-Counseling offers. I add that many people may not have these abilities when they begin the practice, but as they maintain the practice they become fully self-responsible and learn the power and joy of being self-directed. These are some of the gifts Co-Counseling gives the practitioner.

Then I invite everyone to stand and unite in a closing circle. We join hands, close our eyes, and focus on our breathing. After a couple of breaths I ask people to open their eyes and look around the circle to appreciate everyone who has shared the evening with them. "Look at each other; really look!" I encourage. I talk about how this circle is a way to consciously close our gathering. We are moving from the sacred space we created at the beginning of the evening back into the ordinary world. I invite people to say their names (loudly and proudly) and a validation. When that round is complete, I invite them to state something they are taking with from the evening. I remind people to get hugs if they so choose after the circle ends. Lastly I remind people of confidentiality.

Part V

The Self-Counselor at Work

Prologue

The key to Co-Counseling is the session. Within the session two individuals work together, alternating time as self-counselor and co-counselor. The person in the role of co-counselor supports the self-counselor according to a mutually agreed-upon contract. Being fully self-responsible and self-directed, the person in the role of the self-counselor is free to do what she wants and how she wants to do it. Normally this person works to gain clarity on some facet of her life and, with this clarity, makes decisions. The only restriction is no physical violence toward the self, others, or property. Other than this restriction, the person's imagination, the contract, and time are the only constraints.

Chapter 34

Fictionalized Co-Counseling Sessions

Always scrub your soul clean
Don't let it become infected
With old lies and half truths

In a Fundamentals training people do session after session, experiencing in real time what transpires in a session. In this way they come to feel and know the dynamics of being the self-counselor and co-counselor. They begin to internalize various aspects of the roles and learn new techniques and skills as they are presented. I have been discussing most of these aspects, but the reality of the ebb and flow of a session is still missing.

Unless you have done Co-Counseling, some of what has been presented may seem abstract. The information presented so far provides a conceptual framework for a session as well as detailed explanations of the ideas, processes, techniques, and skills used. Now I want to provide a sense of what happens within actual Co-Counseling sessions.

What follows are three imaginary sessions with imaginary people. They have been created out of my knowledge of what happens in sessions. They are not complete sessions, but they illustrate some of what can transpire during a sessions.

There are two techniques used in these sessions that have not been discussed. The first is *interventions,* and the second is *pillow work.* Interventions are short, directive statements used by the co-counselor to move the self-counselor deeper into his work.* When the self-counselor proposes the contract at the beginning of his time he states whether or not he wants interventions. If he does, he specifies the level of interventions he wants—light, moderate, or heavy. Interventions are not advice, interpretation, or feedback. They are based solely in the process and not the content of the self-counselor's work. The self-counselor is free to accept an intervention or ignore it. There should never be a dialogue about an intervention. It is either accepted and used or ignored and forgotten.

---

* Learning to be good at giving interventions takes time and practice. Ideally interventions come from the gut which, which makes them practical and spontaneous, rather than from the brain where the intervention can be contemplated and therefore delivered past its time of usefulness.

Pillow work involves using pillows to represent people in our lives who become part of our work during a session. Rather than talking about the person, we talk directly to him as if he were present. We use the pillow to represent him and speak our truth directly to him. The pillow provides a focus for what we need to say. By talking directly to a person as represented by a pillow, the self-counselor avoids talking "about" the issue he has with the person, which can become story-telling. Talking directly to a pillow allows the self-counselor to access the emotions and feelings attached to the situation. Pillows can represent anything the self-counselor wants, including parts of himself like his heart, gut, or head, or ideas, animals, and inanimate objects. Pillows are also used during the release of emotions.

SCENARIO #1

In a large, fancy living room a man and woman are sitting on the floor facing each other. They are about three feet apart. The man is in the role of the self-counselor. When he set his contract, he specified he wanted caring-aware-attention and eye contact; facial affect was all right, but he wanted no touch and no interventions. He also

202

asked for a warning five minutes before his time as self-counselor ended. He is sitting on a pillow, and she is on a *backjack*. He talks about negative thoughts that pop up in his head.

"I've been cocounseling for five years and feel like I've done so much work, yet these damn thoughts are always popping up in my head."

Suddenly he pauses, moving his head up and down as if approving of an inner thought, and says with a smile: *"I know it's not "always," but lately it seems that they are always yapping, and it really gets me aggravated."*

The tone of his voice changes, *"At a workshop a couple of months ago the facilitators called these voices "negative defaults." They kept emphasizing that the voices were programmed into our brains when we were kids and we aren't responsible for them. They run automatically . . . ."*

He pauses, closes his eyes, takes several breaths, and says with a laugh, *"I know it's my mother's words, but it's my voice."*

He puts his face into has hands, lets out a deep sigh, and continues softly. *"She's been dead three years now, and the irony is, toward the end of her life, she never said these things to me. In fact, she said just the opposite; but I keep hearing the old voices from when I was a kid."*

Stopping, he closes his eyes and sighs.

When he continues, his voice is stronger, *"What they said in that workshop was right. These are clearly old default settings that just don't apply any more, but they keep happening."*

Opening his eyes wide and looking right at the co-counselor he asserts; *"I'm not lazy. I get my work done. I make a good living. I'm not rich, but I get by just fine. We have a nice house."*

He stops suddenly, looks away from the co-counselor, and rocks back and forth on his pillow, clearly thinking. Then sitting straight up, he shakes his head from side to side, lets out another sigh, and looks back at the co-counselor. He smiles a big, silly smile.

"You know, I realize I have started saying these things to my kids." Still smiling, he pauses; then in a firmer voice he says, *"I've got to find some different ways to say things to my kids when I don't think they are taking care of themselves or doing the things they should be doing around the house."*

"Oh God. There I go with the word 'should'. I want my kids to succeed, but I don't want to make them wrong because they aren't perfect.

Shaking his head, he adds, *"God knows, I'm not perfect."*

With a sigh he repeats, *"I'm not perfect. I'm not perfect. I'm not perfect."*

Again there is silence.

"Maybe that's why the voices keep coming up—to remind me I'm not perfect. Maybe that's what my mom was all about. Reminding me I wasn't perfect and that I could do better. That I still had room to grow."

Closing his eyes and settling down on his cushion, he says in a soft voice, "Thanks, mom. Thanks."

Raising his voice and opening his eyes, he continues. *"You know, I haven't thought of her for a while. I miss her, and I miss her being such a great grandmother for my kids. She was our baby sitter, and when she baby-sat she always showed up with dinner for us. My wife and I really appreciated that. We could come home from work and not rush around and make dinner before we went out."*

Pausing thoughtfully, he says in a quieter voice, *"You know, we haven't gone out as much since she died. Maybe those negative voices in my head are to remind me to think of her. I miss her. The kids miss her."*

Softening his voice even more, he says, *"I do miss her. So maybe its important that those critical voices keep popping up. They do make me stop and think about what I'm doing* [pause] *and they make me think of my mother. So maybe those voices are a good thing. Maybe my issue is that I always get angry when I hear them. Maybe I just need to accept them and stop being angry when I hear them. Maybe I just need to accept them and thank them for showing up and reminding me to think about what I am doing and, maybe, to think about my mother."* Strengthening his voice, he asserts knowingly; *"The things we resist, persist. So if I stop resisting these voices, they might just go away, and then I might start thinking of my mother in a less critical way."*

"There are five minutes left," his partner interjects.

After a hesitation, he continues, *"I love the fact her critical voice keeps happening. I love the fact her critical voice keeps happening,"* he repeats a couple more times in a loud, sarcastic voice.

Then he starts repeating his contradiction in a softer and quieter voice. You can hear the sarcasm leaving and a sadness coming into his voice.

Suddenly he says, *"My mother wasn't perfect, but she tried her best to do what she thought was right for me. I know she did the best she could. I've worked hard and forgiven her for how she treated me. I know she wanted the best for me and I do love her, but I don't need her critical voice in my head."*

He stops talking, closes his eyes, and after taking several deep breaths says, *"I love my mother . . . maybe hearing those critical statements is simply a way I remember her."*

He sits back silently with his eyes still closed. *"Maybe if I take the time to think of her in a positive way, these negative thoughts might go away. Somewhere I'm still fighting her."* He hesitates and, when he continues he starts slightly shaking his head up and down, *"I'm going to do that. I'm going to take time to think of my mother in a positive way."*

Opening his eyes, he says thoughtfully, *"That feels good."*

His tone brightens and he sits up straight throwing his shoulders back. *"I have to tag this work,"* he says with a smile on his face. *"I am going to spend some time in my next session thinking positive thoughts about my mom. That'll be different. There are good things buried in here,"* he indicates pointing at his chest.

Suddenly there is a beeping sound, and the co-counselor reaches out and takes a small timer in her hand and silences the beeping.

"What else are you going to take from the session?" his session partner asks.

"Well, I'm taking the life action that I can motivate my kids without using my mother's negatives. I don't want to wire their brains like my brain was wired," he says with a smile on his face.

"Do you need any present time?" she asks.

"Yea, one or two."

She then asks him to name four square objects in the room. She keeps looking at him as he looks around the room naming different objects. When he gets to four, she asks him to name five states bordering Canada He rattles them off and says he is back and would like a hug.

They both get up on their knees and hug each other for what may seem like a long time. When the hug ends, they both stand and silently walk around. He says he has to go to the bathroom and walks out of the room.

When he comes back, the woman is sitting on the floor facing his empty cushion.

He sits down and she speaks assertively. *"I want forty minutes of your caring-aware-attention. I want eye contact. Facial affect is fine, but no touch for now and only light interventions."*

He nods agreement, picks up the timer, sets it, and asks if she would like a five-minute warning. She says *"yes,"* and he starts the timer, putting it on the floor where they both can see it.

"I think I'll start with some new and goods. I'm Charlene, and my new and good is my new assistant at work. I'm Charlene, and my new and good is the beautiful sunset yesterday. I'm Charlene, and my new and good is being here and cocounseling. I'm Charlene, and my new and good is a phone call from my daughter."

Her voice is animated as she flows from one new and good to the next; then changing the tone of her voice, she says:

"What's on top is the new person at work. He is really competent and thorough. I gave him a stack of invoices to go through to check against the computer log of work completed and paid for, and he found three where the dates didn't match. I love it. Everything I've given him to do he just goes right through it, and if he doesn't understand, he asks me really good questions until he knows exactly what I want. Now I can focus on the work I should be doing rather than worrying about whether the work I pass on is done right. It is so good to be able to trust him to do his job right. I feel so relieved not to have to keep worrying about the work of my assistant. I should have fired the woman who worked for me a year ago. It feels so good to relax."

Raising her arms over her head, she says in a loud, clear voice, *"I celebrate my new assistant. I celebrate that he thinks* (emphasizing the work 'thinks') *and he is competent* (emphasizing the word 'competent') *and I don't have to worry about work being done right anymore."*

"What's the feeling?" her partner intervenes.

"RELIEF!! I feel so good. I feel . . ."

210

She hesitates for what seems like an instant.

He intervenes again. *"What's the thought?"*

"The thought is it feels so good to trust people again," she says with a long sigh. "It feels so good trusting again."

"Say 'I feel'," her partner intervenes.

"I feel so good trusting he'll do a good job." She sighs again, and her whole body relaxes. "I feel so good trusting him. It makes my life so much easier." She sits quietly for a moment and then smiles, saying, *"I like trusting people. I like trusting people."* The smile gets bigger.

At this point, her voice changes, becoming much more serious as she starts talking about some friends whom she has stopped trusting

SCENARIO #2

Two men are sitting on chairs in a kitchen facing each other. The man in the self-counselor role is talking while the other is looking at him with a soft, open expression. The man speaking is talking about issues with his wife. He seems very relaxed as he speaks, as if he is very familiar with the subject. In his contract he stated that he wanted "moderate interventions."

"I know she doesn't mean to be negative about my work, and I don't bring in the money I used to, but the economy is bad and people don't have the money to pay me any more. I'm taking on pure carpentry jobs, but it's not my passion. And I'm sure on some level she resents having to go back to work while our daughters are still in school."

He becomes quiet for a while and says, *"Things are going to turn around. I know that. Things are going to get better, and we will survive."*

The co-counselor, who has been clearly and solely focused on the man as he speaks, intervenes: *"Repeat that."*

"We will survive."

"Again," the partner says.

"We will survive," repeats the man. *"We will survive."*

212

Then spontaneously he starts singing, *"We will get by,"* dragging out the last syllable. *"We will survive."*[15]

He breaks out into a big smile and says, *"That's a song from my favorite band. Marcia and I used to go to all their concerts whenever they were any place near here."*

He pauses, and then says reflectively; *"Maybe Marcia and I need to go out to a few concerts again, and maybe we can take our daughters."* He goes on about the idea and ends up saying he will bring it up with Marcia. *"We need to go out. I know Marcia will say we can't afford it, but we can find the money. We need to stop worrying about our problems!"*

He pauses, moving his head up and down, then continues. *"We need to go out and have some fun again and stop being bogged down in money worries before it kills our relationship."*

"By when?" the co-counselor asks.

"I have a couple of jobs coming up, and I'm going to set some money aside for us all to go out." He pauses and takes a couple of breaths. *"Damn it, that's what I'm going to do."*

"*By when?*" the co-counselor repeats.

"*By the end of the month.*"

"*When are you going to talk with Marcia?*", the co-counselor inserts.

"*Tonight, damn it. Tonight, after dinner.*"

Do you want me to call you tomorrow and check up on you?"*

"Yeah, that sounds good."

Raising his arms over his head and looking up at the ceiling he celebrates his new life action and expresses his joy about him and Marcia going out and having some fun.

Suddenly he stops, and a big grin lights up his face. He begins recounting an incident involving the owner of the house where he is working and the person's dog. He starts laughing as he tells the story, acknowledging he didn't feel comfortable laughing while the incident was going on. The man had hired him and could fire him.

---

* "This whole series of interventions from the first "By when?" are part of the emphasis on action-planning, the purpose of which is to take the ideas and thoughts in the session directly into the daily reality.

"Man have I become so damn scared about money!" He pauses, *"I've got to lighten up."*

"Repeat that."

"I've got to lighten up. I've got to lighten up," he says and then gets up off the chair and starts to do a little dance. There is a huge smile on his face. *"I've got to lighten up."* He starts singing; "we shall get by," dragging out the last note. He continues singing as he moves around the kitchen.

"We will survive!" he shouts pumping his fists into the air.

Meanwhile the co-counselor has stood up and is watching, keeping his eyes steadily on the man's eyes as he sings and dances.

SCENARIO #3

In a small room two women are sitting on the floor in front of a couch, facing each other holding hands. The self-counselor is a younger woman

215

talking about how she is feeling disrespected and demeaned by an older male teacher in her school because she looks so young. The woman in the co-counselor role is looking at her with soft, inquisitive eyes and holding her hands as she goes on about her frustration with the teacher who just brushes by her as if she doesn't exist.

The contract here is for intensive interventions.

"*Tell him how you feel when he treats you like this*," the co-counselor says, grabbing a pillow and putting it next to the woman.

The young woman turns, looks at the pillow, and starts addressing the other teacher as if he were sitting on the pillow.

"*I can't stand the way you just walk by me as if I don't exist. You self-righteous bastard.*" Her voice is rising, and her face is turning red.

Her partner now puts several pillows on top of each other and says, "*Put your anger here,*" pointing to the pile of pillows.

The young woman turns and starts pounding the pillows. She raises her arms over her head and

216

strikes the pillows surprisingly hard with her fists. She continues hitting the pillows while looking at the pillow she had been talking to and says, *"This is how angry I feel when you ignore me. I'm as good a teacher as you, if not better. Who do you think you are, you bastard!"*? Saying this she starts hitting the pillows even harder, yelling, *"You bastard, you bastard!"**

Suddenly she drops her head onto the pile of pillows and begins crying, saying in a soft voice; *"You bastard, I am just as good as you; just as good as you. I'm just as good as you."*

Her partner, who has been looking at her with compassion as she was hitting the pillows, now places one hand on the weeping woman's back and says, *"Let it all out, Lois. Stay with it. Let it out."*

After what seems like a long time, the self-counselor stops crying and becomes quiet. The co-counselor rubs her back a bit and then sits back up facing where the woman had been

---

* In doing what is called "cushion work," the self-counselor never strikes the cushion representing a person. To do that would be to commit an act of "virtual violence" toward the person. The anger a person releases is her anger at what the person has done or is doing. In discharging the anger on a separate set of cushions the self-counselor can release the anger while showing the person in a virtual manner just how angry they feel when the person acts in the offensive manner.

217

sitting. Slowly the young woman sits back up, and the two join hands again. *"Oh god, that feels good. I'm so tired of people treating me like a kid."*

"Where else has this happened?"

"It happens all the time," the young woman says as she lets out a low moan and collapses onto the pile of pillows in front of her, sobbing loudly.

The co-counselor again puts a hand on the woman's back and says: ***"Let it out, Lois. Let it all out."***

The young woman cries deeply for a while and then sits up and says: *"I am so tired of being treated like I'm a kid, like I don't know anything simply because I look young."*

Her partner has given her a box of tissues, which the young woman uses to wipe her eyes and blow her nose.

"I'm not going to take it any more," she suddenly says. *"I deserve people's respect."*

The co-counselor immediately says; *"Say it again."*

The woman in the self-counselor role repeats, *"I deserve people's respect. I deserve people's respect. I deserve people's respect!"* Her voice growing stronger each time she says it.

The co-counselor intervenes pointing to the single pillow that Lois had been talking to before. *"Now tell him how you feel."*

The young woman turns to the pillow and starts addressing the man in a quiet, strong voice. *"I don't want to hate you, but I want your respect. I deserve your respect."*

"Say it again."

"I want your respect. I deserve your respect . . . I deserve your respect."

"Again."

"I deserve your respect," Lois says with a deeper, more controlled voice.

"How does it feel to say that?"

"It feels good."

"Say it again."

"I deserve your respect."

"How do you feel?"

"I feel good. I feel good." Then, as she repeats, *"I feel good,"* her voice keeps growing stronger, changing from a tone of petitioning to one of confidence. *"I want and deserve your respect."* Then after a pause: *"I need to talk with him."*

*"Do you want to rehearse what you want to say to him?"**

"Hmmm." Shifting around a bit and sitting up taller, Lois turns toward the cushion representing the male teacher and says, *"Jack, do you have a couple of minutes? I'd like to talk with you. I've been feeling frustrated since the beginning of the school year because I feel you've been ignoring me. I'm a good person*

---

* Many times a person rehearses what she needs to say to someone in a difficult situation so she can say exactly what she wants and how she wants to say it. Often during these "rehearsals," a lot of emotion can come out, reflecting the emotional distress of the self-counselor. By letting out the emotions while rehearsing what she wants to say, the self-counselor eventually becomes able to say exactly what she wants to say without getting carried away by her emotions. This is called "rehearsing the future."

and a good teacher, and I'd like you to stop ignoring me. We're both teachers in the same school. "

The co-counselor jumps in: *"Would you like me to do a role play?"*

The self-counselor never stops talking to the person represented by the pillow, completely ignoring the intervention. *"I know you've been here for years and I am new, but maybe we can find things to share about what's going on here in the school. "*

"Do you have a life action here?" The co-counselor asks."

"I need to talk to him. I still have lots of anger in me but I can do it."

"By when?" her partner asks.

"By the end of school on Friday."

"Do you want me to call you Friday evening and check with you about how it went?"

"I would love for you to call," the self-counselor replies. *"I want to practice what I want to say to him. "* With this she turns to the pillow she has

been addressing, looks at it for a time, and then reaches out and turns it over, saying as an aside: *"I need to believe he has a positive side to him."* With this she begins talking to the flipped over pillow in a calm, strong voice she has yet to use in this session.

Chapter 35

Examining the Sessions

Beaming shining human
Half covered by the past . . .
Emerging
Stumbling toward peaceful joy

In the role of the self-counselor, people work on any-thing they want, in any way they want. The object of the work is to gain clarity on the subject matter being explored and, with this clarity, move toward some desired goal. Being totally self-responsible and self-directed, people have complete freedom to follow what calls them. The only restriction is no physical violence toward the self, others, or property. Other than this restriction and the contract with the co-counselor, imagination and time are the only constraints.

After establishing a contract with the co-counselor, you, as self-counselor, are completely in charge of what you do with your time. You are totally self-directed. You may work on some issue confronting you in your life. You may work to release emotions building up inside or may do regression work to uncover the source of a pattern keeping you in constant crisis. You may sit and reflect on your life or celebrate how great things are. You might move away from your planned work based on a sudden insight and follow an unknown path guided only by what your body gives you through free association. You might simply cease talking and meditate, ask yourself Bryon Katie's four questions, or contemplate ideas of Deepak Chopra, Carolyn Myss, Brené Brown, Joseph Campbell, or other wise people whose thoughts can spark creative thinking. You may walk around, dance while humming a tune only you can hear, sing, draw, sculpt, or receive a massage. Co-Counseling gives you the gift of being in charge of what you do and how you do it. This self-directed freedom is part of what makes Co-Counseling such a unique healing and self-empowering modality.

As you develop a regular practice of cocounseling, you grow to understand and appreciate your life as a never-ending stream of conscious decision-making. There is no *right way* to do a session; yet as you examine different issues you may find yourself running through a logical sequence of questions similar to the following:

   a.   How is this affecting my life?
   b.   Who are the major players?

   c. What is my part?

   d. What are my feelings about what is happening?

   e. How can I resolve the problem?

The people in the three scenarios presented in the last chapter illustrate how different people use their time in the role of the self-counselor. They begin by setting a contract with their co-counselors emphasizing the type of interventions they want. Then they jump into their work. Their goals, as different as they may be, are to resolve in a positive manner whatever situations they are working on. This is the basic work that has sustained Co-Counseling as an alternative therapy for over forty years. People actively apply the skills and techniques learned in Fundamentals training to explore, understand, and take action on aspects of their lives that are causing them unhealthy stress. This formulation of Co-Counseling matches the expectations most people have when they take the training. This is the vision and stated purpose articulated on Co-Counseling websites around the world. People come to Co-Counseling to actively move and improve their lives.

THE FIRST SCENARIO:

The man in the role of self-counselor in the first scenario has asked for a no-intervention contract, but note that he continually intervenes in his own work. He is completely self-directed. He is aware of the issue with the voices. He explores ideas that came from a workshop he attended, which is a standard practice for cocounselors.* He uses the ideas and makes a connection directly to his mother, who died three years ago. He then starts to examine his feelings for his mother, and promises through the use of a *tag* (a mental note to the self) that he will do this in his next session. He also asserts that he will no longer say the things to his kids that his mother used to say to him and makes a humorous note about wiring his kids' brains.

His session revolves around the central subject of the voices he hears in his head but jumps from his mother, to his kids, to the workshop, back to the voices, and back again to his mother. The man has established a sacred relationship with his body. He not only hears, but also trusts, the messages his body gives him. He is using what in Co-Counseling is called *free association*. He follows the messages as if they were interventions, and

---

* Many people attend workshops and then head directly back into their busy lives. They never take the time to explore the information presented, what it might mean for them, and how they might fit it into their lives.

in fact they are the body's way of guiding him to what he needs to work on—his relationship with has mother.

In the second part of the scenario, the woman, who has asked for light interventions, is totally involved in her work life. She is celebrating the relief she feels having a great new assistant she can trust. Then, an intervention brings attention to a thought she had about *trust*. The thought, which might have slipped by if it wasn't for the intervention, changes the focus of her work from her job into her personal life. As we leave the scenario, she is beginning to work on the issue of trust with her friends.

By starting with "what's on top," she freed herself from the concerns of her work life, which probably dominate a good part of her thinking. She can now concern herself with other elements of her life. The co-counselor, being completely *out with* her, noticed a hesitation in her voice as the trust issue with her friends passed through her brain. By simply saying, "thought," he points her to the thought, and it changes the focus of her work. She then moves away from her concern about her job and into her disturbing situation involving friendships and trust. We don't know what she does with this new work, but we know she has touched an essential part of her humanity–her relationship with her friends.

THE SECOND SCENARIO:

We join the session as the person in the self-counselor role is reflecting on the hard times he and his wife are experiencing in their marriage due to money issues. Worrying about money, the future, and his family has dominated his thinking; and the more he thinks, the more the issues seem to spiral out of control. Speaking the worries out loud stops the negative spiraling. As he talks about them, he can look at the issues more objectively. This is what many people do in their sessions. They escape the incessant mental rehashing of problems by speaking them out loud. By doing this, the problems become stationary and can be logically examined and acted upon.

He says he believes they will survive the issues facing them. The co-counselor intervenes, simply suggesting he "repeat that" and the self-counselor repeats "we will survive" several times and then bursts into song, noting the line is from a song his favorite band sings. That thought brings him to an idea that might help the relationship. He and his wife need to go out and stop worrying about money. He pauses, asserts the idea is good, and states he is going to ask his wife out. The co-counselor asks the action-planning question, "By when?" When the self-counselor stumbles around a bit, the co-counselor again asks, "By when?" He gets an answer, but pushes. "When are you going to ask your wife?" He then gets an immediate response. The co-counselor next asks if the self-counselor would like to be called as a checkup on how the asking went. The self-counselor agrees and then goes off on a rant about how even he has become so serious about money that he is afraid to be spontaneous. He says he has to lighten up. Then suddenly he gets up and starts dancing and singing while the co-counselor simply sits and watches.

The man is stressed, and the simple intervention, *repeat that* gets him to pause. He starts to free-associate and soon winds his way to the new idea, which cut through his pessimistic thinking. There is no way he could have arrived logically at this idea.

229

THE THIRD SCENARIO:

The young woman asked for heavy interventions, and the co-counselor agreed. When we joined the session, we found the co-counselor actively involved in the self-counselor's work. She is putting a pillow in front of the self-counselor inviting her to tell the older teacher, who is ignoring her, exactly how she feels. As the self-counselor does so, her voice rises in anger. The co-counselor puts a stack of pillows next to the young woman and suggests she "put her anger here," pointing to the stack of pillows. The young woman turns and starts pounding the stack of pillows and continues pounding them, thereby releasing her pent-up anger. Then she collapses onto the pillows and cries, acknowledging her frustration at continually being treated as a kid because she looks so young. After she stops crying, she lies on the pillows for a while; sitting up, she suddenly states she deserves people's respect.

The beauty of Co-Counseling is that it provides a safe place to explore, release, and make friends with your emotions regardless of their source or intensity. The young woman in this scenario perceives her fellow teacher as a dismissive person who is attacking her self-worth and responds internally with anger, which is the natural response to having a personal boundary violated. She is a teacher and believes she should be respected as one. That is a boundary, and it has been violated. Her anger is natural, but what is she going to do with it?

The session gives her the safe space to release her anger, but notice that after she does so, a well of sadness appears. Why? Because this same issue centering around a lack of respect has happened over and over again in her life, and it stirs up old sadness inside her. She is tired of people continually judging her as *less than* because she looks so young. For her, what is happening at school with the other teacher is just another occurrence of this old problem. She needs to release her sadness before focusing on how to address her situation with the older teacher. She does this by letting her body collapse onto the pillows, where she can fully feel and release her sadness through an outpouring of tears and the sounds of sadness.

In Co-Counseling we have found emotions come in layers, and when you release one emotion, another one may be buried immediately underneath the first. This second emotion is old and familiar, and has probably been repressed for years. Now that it has been uncovered, the person can feel it, explore it, and release it by physically discharging the emotion and the pent-up energy stored in it. When we release this repressed energy, we can gain a whole new perspective on ourselves or the situation in which it was hidden, as the young teacher does when she suddenly starts to assert that she deserves people's respect.

She repeats this several times, and as she reclaims her sense of personal power, the co-counselor directs her to tell the older teacher how she feels. This time the woman speaks without being emotional. She comes to an understanding as she is speaking that she needs to talk to the other teacher. Her session partner suggests she rehearse what she wants to say, and she does. Then the co-counselor asks her the standard action-planning questions—*by when* is she going to talk to the other teacher and *would she like support* in the form of a phone call inquiring how the conversation turned out. The assurance of a simple phone call gives the young woman the knowledge and confidence she will be supported no matter how her interaction with her fellow teacher works out. We leave the scenario as the self-counselor gladly agrees to receive a call.

Chapter 36

Moving beyond Shame

To tell or not to tell
To speak truth or not speak truth
Are there really choices

In our fast-paced, demanding, and sometimes annoying world, many people rush from one event to another without taking the time to understand the thoughts, feelings, and emotions bubbling within them. People go to clubs, bars, and cafés where they talk about their lives, the lives of people they know, public figures, and characters in television and movies. In these social situations people seldom go very deeply into their own lives but often engage in extensive analyses of others. We may speak about our issues and concerns with friends, but we seldom take the time to fully explore the details or look at our part in these situations. We end up walking on eggshells, being super conscious of what we say and how we say it. Do we want to talk about our loneliness or guilt feelings concerning our behavior in our last relationship? Do we want people to know exactly how much we hate our boss but stay at our job because we are too scared to be without a job?

Our social-survival skills (patterns) steer us away from bringing up things we are ashamed of because we will be exposing ourselves as flawed and possibly be rejected by those who know our flaws. We become anxious and distressed when we even approach these areas of our lives. We are afraid to disturb the surface layer of peacefulness around us, yet our efforts to stay safe rob us of spontaneity and a robust energetic engagement with life.

The issues and concerns we don't talk about cause us stress and interfere with our ability to think clearly. We want to relieve ourselves of the stress by solving our problems by ourselves. Most of us tend to do our problem solving and self-analysis in our heads where our thinking whips around and around and seldom ever becomes clear. The thoughts recycle endlessly, causing more and more distress, or become the basis of fantasy, which also cycles and recycles without solving anything. All of this thinking can take people further and further away from the actual reality from where they started. After countless trips through the swirling eddies of the mind, people grab at any solution that seems even remotely feasible in order to stop from drowning in their own thoughts. The energy expended worrying or fantasizing about an issue prior to reaching a solution doesn't leave much energy for well-conceived planning to bring the decision into reality. Many of these "solutions" end up discarded when they work poorly or not at all. This leads people back into their heads, where they spend more and more time disengaged from the physical world in which they live. If you stay in your head, you might as well stay in bed, which can happen as people get overwhelmed with life and become depressed, which leads to doctors, pills, and a life sentence in a pharmaceutical prison.

Co-Counseling offers a sacred space where we step outside of our socially constricted world and contemplate *out loud* the issues, problems, and joys in our daily lives. We begin our time in the self-counselor role by emptying our brain of its constant chatter through the use of What's on Top. This stops the cycling and recycling of thoughts that lead us away from grounded reality. Then either by a predetermined choice or free association, we begin to focus on a particular piece of work needing our attention and time.

Many beginning cocounselors, however, stay away from issues they hold as shameful, despite having heard the Fundamentals trainer say the co-counselor who is sitting right in front of them, listening to their every word, is *out with* them and not evaluating, judging, or trying to fix them. This has been repeated over and over again, along with the idea that everything they say is confidential. Yet our social-survival pattern steers us away from bringing up areas of our lives we hold in shame.

Brené Brown in her book *The Gift of Imperfection* says

> Shame is the intensely painful feeling or experience of believing that we are flawed and therefore unworthy of love and belonging.[16]

So it makes sense that new cocounselors don't talk about intensely painful areas of their lives they have associated with shame. They want to be accepted and have a hard time believing that the co-counselor, who is giving them the energy of caring-aware-attention, will not judge them negatively if they reveal sources of their unworthiness.

We naturally seek approval and want to be liked. Just because the trainer said the people in the co-counselor role are not there to judge, evaluate, or fix us, do we really believe it? Can we really trust them? Everything in our history says, "B*e cautious, you don't know these people.*" We are in a new environment with new people and want to feel accepted, and so we are cautious about what we speak about as the self-counselor. Our social-survival pattern is still solidly in place.

After several sessions you begin to believe *confidentiality* holds in a session because you are maintaining it and no one has ever brought up anything you've said in a session. Amazing! Because of your experience in the co-counselor role, you start to understand a person in that role can be *out with* the self-counselor without judging or evaluating. You start to feel the self-counselor across from you trusts you as she speaks openly about her life, and this makes it easier for you to trust her.

As your willingness to trust evolves, you begin to speak more and more honestly about your life. The degree to which you have shame attached to a matter and are willing to talk openly about the matter is a good measure of your sense of personal safety. Shame seems to be the critical barrier keeping all of us from fully disclosing details about our lives in front of others. The more shame we have regarding anything, the less likely we are to talk about it. When we first begin cocounseling, we may be willing to talk about items we don't feel much shame about, but shy away from anything deeper. The more we cocounsel, the more willing we are to speak about things we hold as deeply shameful. As we continue to talk about them, the shame attached to them lessens. Speaking them out loud forces us to clarify and objectify that which we hold as shameful, thereby gaining a new perspective on them. The new perspective allows us to examine the things we hold as shameful and explore the origins of the shame itself. In bringing up matters buried in layers of shame, we deepen our work and lighten our life.

Chapter 37

The *Rubber Duck*

Wealthiness of the mind
is
having choices
real choices
Broad road to a sweet life

In Co-Counseling sessions participants need to step out of the habits they have developed to participate in the world of social conversation. In them we actively stay aware of how our thoughts and ideas are being received by those listening to us. We consciously keep our thoughts moving in linear progressions, connecting everything we say so the listener can easily follow our train of thought. We want to be understood. We speak in short bursts and then rest as another person speaks. As they speak we analyze what is being said in relation to what we have said and what we are going to say. The participants seldom consciously agree upon the direction and flow of the conversation. It simply evolves, spinning and twirling from one subject to another.

Conversations are a give and take between and among people who want to be heard. Most speakers in conversations are talking so that others can know what they are thinking. Conversations are about communication and connection. The focus is outward, and if we become enamored of our own thoughts, we may be labeled egotistical, vain, or boastful. Conversations are rarely the place for self-analysis, prolonged concentration on one subject, or displays of emotions, except symbolically in words such as "I'm really angry," or "That makes me sad." Conversations seldom need meaningful endings. The human needs for self-expression and understanding fuel conversations, while the desire for friendships and acceptance underlie them. Social conversations build the common ground of ideas and values among the participants cementing their friendships and communities. They are critical to our existence as social beings.

What happens in a session, however, is not about friendship. In each of the senarios in chapter 33, we have no idea whether the two people involved in a session are friends or not. And it makes no difference. The session is not a social conversation. From an outside perspective a session may look like the self-counselor is talking to the co-counselor. This, however, is not the case. The self-counselor is talking so he can hear what he is saying, so he can pay attention to his own thoughts—so he can get in touch with his own wisdom and use this wisdom to counsel himself.

The essence of being a self-counselor is to pay attention to what we are saying while we are saying it. Co-Counseling has nothing to do with act of conversation. In fact, all of the patterns we developed beginning in childhood that guide us in social conversation have to be ignored as we act in the role of the self-counselor. When a person first begins learning the role during the Fundamentals training, he invariably begin speaking directly to the co-counselor. He carefully includes details to guide the co-counselor in his understanding. Further, the person speaking is probably concerned with being accepted, having just met the person listening to him. This is what we have always done. The new person's brain recognizes a *social-conversation scenario* the moment he sits down to talk in front of another person. The social-conversation pattern automatically starts running. To be a self-counselor, however, we can't be concerned with speaking to be heard and understood by the co-counselor. Though this may seem strange; it is essential to getting the benefits of Co-Counseling. So one of the first goals in a Fundamentals training is for a new person to learn to keep conscious focus on his own words and feelings, which is not easy. In a situation that clearly looks like a social conversation, the new person needs to stop and develop new patterns (new neuro-networks) appropriate to the role of the self-counselor. To do this we need to stay conscious of exactly what we are doing every time we sit in the role of the self-counselor and not let our social-conversation patterns define our actions.

The key to developing this new pattern is to stop focusing on the co-counselor and focus solely on the thoughts and feelings running around within us. Co-Counseling is about pulling thoughts from the recesses of our brains and engaging them out loud. I invite people to consider the amount of time and conscious energy they spend thinking about their daily struggles as well as the past and future. This time may be considered problem solving, planning, speculating, contemplating, daydreaming, or fantasizing. The truth is, no matter what we call it, we spend a considerable amount of time in our heads, thinking, and it is the most solitary and, sometimes lonely, of all activities.

The more we think about an issue inside the whirlpool of our brains, the greater the likelihood of frustration building to the point of boiling over. We instinctively know that keeping these thing bottled up inside ourselves doesn't work—it doesn't solve any of our problems. Sometimes we may simply dump our stuff onto friends telling them we just need to get this off of our chests. We don't need them to understand what we are saying or why we are saying it. We just use them to speak out loud the chaos of thoughts boiling within us. On other occasions we simply burst forth and talk to ourselves because the frustration of keeping our thoughts inside has become unbearable. We do this even though we know talking out loud to ourselves is associated with "crazy people." We all speak out loud to ourselves at some time and know it relieves some of the pressure and stress within us. But because of the only-crazy-people-talk-to-themselves concept, most people only talk to themselves or rant or explode in a torrent of emotions or words in places where they will not be heard —in their cars, bathrooms, bedrooms, or maybe in the woods.

As a kid I would hear my mother talking to herself in the kitchen while cooking dinner. She would have the door to the kitchen closed and would pour out all her problems probably because she had no one to share her truth with. At the time I thought it was funny, but now, realizing her aloneness, it makes me sad.

There is a term in software programing called *rubber ducking*. The term refers to a method programmers use to find solutions to programming problems.[17] The method involves going through the code one line at a time, speaking each line out loud to a little yellow rubber duck. The duck simply sits and does not interrupt the programmer, allowing him to finish his thinking process at whatever pace he needs. And the little yellow rubber duck doesn't have to understand anything being said. So although the programmer is talking in the direction of the rubber duck, he is truly and consciously talking to himself and listening carefully to the words he is speaking.

Talking out loud to the rubber duck allows the speaker to clarify his thoughts and uncover hidden assumptions, while engaging different parts of the brain than when merely thinking about the same ideas. Talking out loud for the explicit purpose of hearing yourself slows down the process of thinking. It also allows us to skip details that would be needed if we were explaining the same idea to another person. We don't have to connect our thoughts to understand ourselves. We can get directly to a central issue without any of the fluff that embellishes conventional conversation.

Similar to a programmer rubber ducking, self-counselors speak into their own listening, speaking to their own ear. So we speak at our own pace in our own private language. By speaking out loud, we increase the chances of initiating new perspectives on what has been running around in our heads. "The simple act of rewording your ideas into a form suitable for speech can often be enough to trigger further thought."[18] Not only do we decide on specific words to express the slippery thoughts running around inside us, but we also string the words together into structures we can understand and respond to. Beyond the structuring of the ideas, we hear the pitch, tone, inflection, passion, and heartache in our voice that doesn't exist while the same words buzz about inside our heads. We give texture to our ideas and, through the texture can recognize the emotional content behind the words, thus helping us see and engage our emotions within the safety of a session. Touching the emotions is another source of inspiration for further thought.

By speaking out loud we activate parts of our brains that are not stimulated when we merely think. The actual process of speaking out loud allows us to recognize our voice in a manner different from hearing anyone else speak. Our spoken words travel through space and arrive in our ears while the vibration of our vocal chords travels up through the skull and activate the hammer, anvil, and stirrup inside the inner ear, amplifying and deepening our words as they are "heard" by the brain. The vibration set up by the vocal chords increases the electrical activity present in the brain while our words are being heard, which may also stimulate the production of new ideas.

As the self-counselor we are paying complete attention to our words while a person stands or sits in front of us. In many ways that person is like the little yellow rubber duck: He never interrupts the flow of ideas, he holds everything done and said in strictest confidentiality, and his presence helps focus our energy. Beyond these three basic tasks, the co-counselor also serves as a witness to the self-counselor's work, validating his work while supplying the energy of caring-aware-attention. So the rubber duck may be great if you are a programmer finding errors in code; but as a human working on your life, the support and energy of a co-counselor is preferable.

In social conversation the value of speaking out loud is lost because the purpose of the speaking is communication and connection. As a new person in Co-Counseling you must learn to listen to yourself when you are in the role of the self-counselor. My advice is to stay focused inside your body. If necessary, close your eyes to blot out the co-counselor. Your work is not about them. Learning to stay focused on your own voice with all its inflections, as well as on the content of what you are speaking, is at the heart of being a self-counselor.

As you tune into yourself you further the process of developing the sacred relationship with yourself that allows for true personal transformation. As you learn to listen to yourself and reflect on what you say, you are developing new neuro-networks that focus attention on your relationship with yourself—your own words, feelings, and emotions. This relationship is essential to becoming your own self-counselor.

Chapter 38

Don't Know—Just Do It

You get your intuition back when you make space for it, when you stop the chattering of the rational mind. The rational mind doesn't nourish you. You assume that it gives you the truth, because the rational mind is the golden calf that this culture worships, but this is not true. Rationality squeezes out much that is rich and juicy and fascinating.

—Anne Lamott, *Bird by Bird*

In the scenarios in the chapter 33, the people are consciously addressing specific issues in their lives. To resolve situations like these requires: (1) understanding both the details and the larger context; (2) determining what part of the responsibility belongs to us, to others, and what part fate plays; (3) separating out the emotional charge from the situation and releasing the emotions to allow for clear decision-making; (4) deciding what we want

247

from the situation; and (5) making and carrying out a plan to get what is wanted. We choose a situation, come to understanding it, decide what we want, and act on the decision. That in a nutshell is what the self-counselor does to clear up personal issues.

We do this work through what Einstein says is the rational mind. We work in a logical fashion—gather facts, examine them, make decisions, and act on the decision. To maximize use of the rational mind, we need to free ourselves of any emotions demanding attention. In Co-Counseling we are not afraid of emotions. We view them as the body's natural response to external events or internal expectations. Unacknowledged emotions, however, drain energy and awareness from the rational mind. Clear thinking becomes almost impossible when we are filled with anger, sadness, fear, or even joy. In Co-Counseling we make friends with our emotions and release them. Once we let them go in the safety of a session, we can think clearly, utilizing our rational mind. In this manner we put one foot in front of another and move forward, knowing we are clearly seeing where we are and what is in front of us. As long as we are alive, new situations and challenges will present themselves to us and we will need to utilize our unencumbered rational mind to guide us.

Too often before I began Co-Counseling I would think and think about a decision I needed to make. I lined up all the facts favoring one outcome on one side and all the facts favoring a second outcome on another; and if there was a third option, I would do the same with that. Then I would weight one side against the other. I wanted clarity in my decision-making, yet sometimes despite lining up all the facts I could not make a clear decision. Ultimately I would make a choice but would not be one hundred per cent sure it was the right choice, so I would not put one hundred per cent of my effort into implementing the decision. Without total commitment my decisions often did not work out, so I ended up scared to make decisions.

After learning Co-Counseling, I used my time in the self-counselor role to make decisions. I would run through pretty much the same scenario I used before I started Co-Counseling, but now I did all of my thinking out loud. I began to gain more clarity about what I wanted by doing this. I started feeling and acknowledging the emotions that lay under my rational thinking. Talking out loud gave me access to the emotional content involved, and I always found layers of such content. I would then engage these emotions till they dissolved and I could clearly see the decision.

By acknowledging and releasing the emotions involved in the decision, I could pause and explore any unconscious patterns operating below the surface of my rational thinking. This often freed the current decisions from past decisions that might not have worked out. As the issue I was working on became free of its emotional component and any unconscious ties to the past, I could use my intelligence to understand the alternative solutions. Speaking out loud allowed new energy to come to the surface, and I could *feel* the energy in each possible course of action. As I came to believe more and more in the sacred relationship with myself, I started to accept one alternative over the others because it felt more right than the others. I began trusting that each decision was the best I could make, and as a result, I became totally committed to following that choice.

A question I have asked myself since I started doing this work is: How do I actually arrive at decisions? The above process seems reasonable and rational. I began to understand very few personal decisions can be made through pure logic. Patterns and emotions play a huge role in all our personal decisions and need to be taken into consideration. The contemplation seems so rational. We lay out the alternatives, scrub them clean of emotional content and old patterns, explore possible outcomes, anticipate the consequences of each outcome, and then—and then?

I heard Zen master Seung Sahn from the Providence Zen center say many times, "Don't know. Just do it!" That is what most of us do. Do I really know what the future holds

250

if I choose one alternative over the other? No! Should I be writing this book or out cross-country skiing? Should I buy this used car over that used car? Should I go to see this movie or that movie? Either choice can be fine, but I need to make the decision to do one or the other. There is neither right nor wrong involved. Each option satisfies a different need and desire, but I cannot do both at the same time. Is there really a logical choice? Don't know. Just do it! And so I make the choice. Then I act on my choice. Don't know. Just do it! And I enjoy myself trusting my choice.

Since no decision can be guaranteed correct at the moment the decision is made, all we can do is believe in the correctness of the decision. Within the sacred space of a Co-Counseling session, I have come to understand that all these decisions are made intuitively. My head may work hard clarifying and organizing the various components of the decision-making process, but the decision will ultimately spring from my gut, which is spontaneous and practical, or from my heart, which is compassionate and wise. In the middle of my contemplation on an issue, I would suddenly know exactly what I was going to do. The decision seemed to made for me as if by magic—like there was no decision to be made.

At other times, however, for all the conscious work I do attempting to arrive at a particular decision, the solution remains elusive. I may return to it over and over again, but there is no clarity. In these cases I have learned to stop worrying about it because the time has not yet come to make the decision. Then, while walking down a street a week later, all of a sudden I know what to do. Our intuition works at its own pace, and we have to give it the space and time it needs. Patience is a virtue we can learn when we are consciously waiting for an answer to a question we have asked ourselves, such as what decision we shall make.

> You do not have to be good.
> You do not have to walk on your knees
> for a hundred miles through the desert
> repenting.
> You only have to let the soft animal of your body
> love what it loves.

> Mary Oliver, "Wild Geese"

What we do in Co-Counseling is create space for our intuition to be heard and respected. We create space for our bodies to come alive and guide us. We give our bodies permission to speak and be heard. We learn to trust the voices speaking from within because we have gotten to know them. We know our voice as it speaks to us. What this has meant for me was that, after years of agonizing over decisions, I found myself trusting my decisions.

Don't Know—Just Do It

While I cannot guarantee the decision will work out the way I envisioned, simply making the decision and acting on it with confidence always feels good and empowering.

Lastly, after the self-counselor accepts the decision that has come to her, she immediately arranges to act on the decision. She can do this because she has a gut-level knowledge that the decision is the right decision. In the scenarios in chapter 33 each self-counselor makes at least one decision that seems to leap forth spontaneously as they are doing their work. In two of the cases, the co-counselors jump in and offer support to the self-counselors in the form of *action-planning.**

Offering to help a session partners carry out decisions is standard practice within a session. When as a co-counselor, I hear the self-counselor make a decision, I immediately ask "by when" which may stimulate more thought on their part or a firming up of the decision. This simple intervention supports the person as she considers moving from thought to action. The self-counselor is then empowered to rethink the decision or act on it with the support of another person—what a powerful gift.

---

* In the scenario where no support was offered, a 'no intervention' contract was in place so the co-counselor did not offer support; but at the end of the session, the self-counselor reminds himself to follow through on the decisions made.

Decision-making and action-planning are essential to moving our lives forward and, therefore, are indispensable parts of what a person does in the self-counselor role. Sometimes the decision made involves accomplishing a goal requiring multiple steps to bring to fruition. In such a case the self-counselor may set up a *life action contract* with another cocounselor in which they work out the details of manifesting the decision together as a team. This requires a more extensive and complex form of planning, which is taught and practiced in the Fundamentals training. This type of long-range planning requires constant adjustment over time, and having a support person who understands both the importance of the goal to the person making it and the details necessary to achieve the goal, makes reaching the goal far easier than doing it by ourselves.

Part VI

The Co-Counselor and the Art of Giving

Prologue

Using Co-Counseling brings understanding and clarity to our lives. We become conscious of patterns that no longer serve us, and we create alternatives to them. After discharging stored repressed emotions, we become friends with them as they arise in us, and use their energy to move our lives forward. We learn to trust our decisions and to act on them appropriately. These are probably the main reasons people take the training and maintain a Co-Counseling practice. But while we are doing all of this wonderful dynamic work, something else is happening. Our lives are changing. Who we are is changing. In this last part of the book we explore the phenomena of personal growth and change.

Chapter 39

Appreciating Ourselves as Human

All life is about us
Let us see commonality
All humans are human

We have such a hard time seeing ourselves as human. We may have the shell and the heart of a human, but we are men and women with consciousness. We exist in a personal universe we create and have control over. We are so much more than an animal, no matter a primate or a mammal. Somehow identifying ourselves with our species name seems to make us something other than, and less than, the wonderful beings we hold ourselves to be.

Ten fingers . . . YES!
Ten toes . . . YES!
My child is ok!
Our baby in ok

What kind of baby?
A girl baby! or maybe
A boy baby!
A bundle of joy . . .
Everything is ok
The baby is fine.
Is it a human baby?
Well . . . yes, dah, of course it is, but
Its my baby . . . MY BABY
It is a Lovely little baby . . .
Not merely human . . . mine . . . Special . . .
Mine
This baby is . . . is . . . Unique
Not just human . . . But mine. MINE!
My baby
My little boy. My little girl. Special!![19]

If someone were to ask you who you are, you would probably not answer "a human." More than likely you would describe your occupation, nationality, religion, color of your skin, sexual orientation, gender choice, or relationship to a particular group of people. The sum total of all the many ways you can identify yourself speaks little about who you are as a person. Yet the categories you choose distinguish you from me and from others while giving you a unique identity. These associations can also connect you with me while separating us from others. You may attribute great meaning to these associations.

And yet, the sum of all these identities leaves much about you as a person unsaid.

Co-Counseling is the perfect forum in which to see others and ourselves as human. From the very beginning of a Fundamentals training, the trainer points out that we are all peers in our humanity. We are all peers in our humanness. Exterior labels have no place in Co-Counseling. The people in a training accept the idea of being peers in their humanity before they start appreciating it on a visceral level. Feeling like peers with others may be a challenge for some people; but when you sit down in a session and you speak your truth to another person, whether you know him or not, and then switch roles and listen to him speaking honestly of his life, the peerness between the two of you starts to become real.

In a small book exploring Co-Counseling and therapy, Rose Evison and Richard Horobin, two of the first CCI Co-Counseling trainers in England, talk about the benefits of working with many people.

> Working with a variety of partners results in exposure to a wide range of human distresses, and the experiential learning that intensive emotional expression does not equate with being bad, mad, or out of control; contrary to the cultural stereotype. Analogously, seeing

260

women expressing anger and men crying, serves
to disrupt deep rooted assumptions concerning
gender differences.[20]

By witnessing many people being honest about their lives,
a person gets to put his life into a perspective that is not
available to people living in the ordinary world or doing
work with a single therapist, counselor, or psychologist. A
person entering Co-Counseling knows his own distresses
and issues; but within the Fundamentals training alone
he is exposed to the problems and issues facing several
other people who appear to be living a regular life in the
ordinary world. Most people in our modern world are
isolated in their struggles, distresses, and emotional pain.
Very few people share the deep hurts they carry around
inside them. After only two or three cocounseling sessions, a person starts to understand that he has stepped
into a world where people share their issues and problems. The new cocounselor quickly learns that having issues and problems is no longer a reason to feel alone.
They are now in a community of people consciously
working to create better lives for themselves.

In chapter 25 I discussed the English concept of the co-
counselor being *out with* the self-counselor and likened
it to meditation. Co-counselors are fully present for the
self-counselors without judging, evaluating, or attempting to fix them. The co-counselor is not thinking; his

brain is quiet, at rest. It has occurred to me many times that what I am doing as the co-counselor is meditating on the person sitting in the self-counselor role, not as an individual, but as a human. In some forms of meditation, a person focuses on a specific mantra or on each individual breath and becomes one with the mantra or the breath. The Sutra of Mindfulness says, "When walking, the practitioner must be conscious that he is walking. When sitting, the practitioner must be conscious that he is sitting. When lying down, the practitioner must be conscious of lying down."[21] In Co-Counseling I focus on a person and I become one with him not as a particular person, but as a human who represents all humans. In this way I start experiencing myself, and the person as human, and that has powerful consequences.

Being fully present as a co-counselor for different people as they describe their specific problems and dilemmas, you begin to see each of them not in his surface identity, but as a human being struggling to live the best life he can. The more people you share sessions with, the stronger your awareness becomes that everyone is human and that all humans struggle.

Often at workshops, I will cocounsel with people I do not know. My lack of specific knowledge about them makes no difference to what I do in the co-counselor role. I know the person in the self-counselor role is a fellow human who desires to live a good life. I know he is not perfect. I know he was raised by parents who were not perfect, just as I was raised by parents who were not perfect. I know he can be in pain and is committed to move his life forward. I know he accepts the culture and the framework of Co-Counseling as taught in a Fundamentals training any place on earth. I don't need to know anything more about the person to be fully present for him and to be a good co-counselor.

Co-Counseling is the only place I know or have heard of that brings us directly into a meaningful connection with our humanity. Most human interactions are based on surface identities, which lead to division, separation, and ultimately conflict among people. It takes time for a person beginning his Co-Counseling practice to make the leap from seeing the person across from him as a unique person working on his life to seeing and accepting him as a human struggling as all humans struggle. There is no "ah ha" moment. The transformation is gradual, and when it happens, there is a powerful sense of connection with the person as human. From this comes a caring and natural compassion for the person that are impossible as long as the person is viewed as a separate unique individual.

By seeing and accepting your session partner as human, you naturally identify with him and in this common identity you get to see and accept *yourself* as human. In doing this you give yourself a great gift because now you are allowing yourself to struggle as all humans struggle—it is in the nature of our being. Seeing yourself as human gives you a new perspective that permits you to detach from the notion that "I've got to be perfect before I can accept myself." This knowledge allows you to shed any guilt or shame you may have attached to making mistakes or not knowing what to do next or being confused. Without the excess baggage of self-criticism, you can more easily rectify a mistake, get clear about what is next, and hop on a path that leads you out of the swamp of confusion.

By silencing the critic in us who demands perfection, we can begin to enjoy mistakes and see them as opportunities to grow. We can laugh at ourselves and the negative voices that pop into our heads whenever we get confused or make a mistake. Then we can discard the pejorative excuse, "What do you expect? She's just human," and adopt the positive idea, "What do you expect? She's wonderfully human."

In accepting ourselves as human, our lives become more stable. No longer do we chastise ourselves for struggling to make decisions. We don't get caught up in the wild fluctuations of living in the world of exterior appearances. We are not weak or confused because we are unsure of which path to take; rather we are wonderfully human. Every human makes mistakes, and the secret is to use the mistake as the basis for learning and growing. There are no perfect humans. We all make mistakes. Self-criticism based on comparisons and expectations withers at our feet when we know ourselves as human. This does not mean letting go of learning about ourselves or working to improve our lives; in fact, it means just the opposite. Now we can go forward without fear. If we make a mistake, we make a mistake and move forward again. The negative judgments we might have had are no longer meaningful. Humans, like all animals, learn from their mistakes and move forward. Living becomes easier.

Chapter 40

Self-Acceptance

Many pieces to life
friends
jobs
home
loves
lovers
money
stimulation
soul rest

Fitting them together
Is the art and craft of living
Being all . . . being one

Many positive elements are implicit when any Co-
Counseling session takes place. A person who wants to
work on her own life initiates the session. When she ask
another person to be her session partner she is making a
clear statement that she trusts this person to support her

as she digs into her life. The second person demonstrates her respect and trust for the first person by agreeing to do the session. Both people show up at the agreed time and probably share a warm, nurturing hug. Together they physically set up the space for the session, make the decision about who will be the self-counselor first, and agree to a contract defining expectations within the session.

Once the session begins, the person in the co-counselor role gives the self-counselor caring-aware-attention while holding her as good to the core. The co-counselor stays fully present for the self-counselor, who may be talking about her children, releasing torrents of anger, celebrating new and goods, or carefully making plans for the future. The self-counselor is fully involved in her work and may not even be aware of the life-enhancing energy being directed at her. Every time she looks up, however, she sees the co-counselor giving her soft-eyed, full attention. The person sitting across from her is looking calmly into her eyes with a warm, accepting gaze. The co-counselor may be touching her physically as well as with the energy of full attention. This focused awareness is alive and active, yet it is not oppressive. It is loving, warm, and respectful.

In Co-Counseling the person in the self-counselor role is counseling herself. She may be resolving a personal conflict, seeking the best way to apologize to a friend for an unkind remark, or examining the origins of a pattern she has been struggling with for months. She may be taking things out of her skeleton closet and talking about them, knowing they are a source of guilt and shame. The self-counselor is honestly examining her life and her world is not collapsing. Witnessing these many facets of her life as they are truthfully revealed, her co-counselor does not turn away in disgust or grimace but simply continues to give her caring-aware-attention. The co-counselor stays fully present holding the self-counselor as good to the core and the self-counselor can see and feel this positive energy flowing in her direction.

At the end of the session, the co-counselor asks the self-counselor if she wants present time and will usually offer a nurturing hug of appreciation and caring. Then the two people switch roles. The person who was the co-counselor moves into the role of the self-counselor and begins to do her work exhibiting complete trust in the person who just finished working. The new self-counselor immediately digs into her life, maybe releasing some anger she is holding or exploring why she has resistance about visiting her mother. The person now in the co-counselor role is giving her caring-aware-attention and accepting the self-counselor as good to the core.

At some point all cocounselors begin to understand that no matter what they disclose about themselves while in the role of the self-counselor, their session partner, when they switch roles, will still trust them to hold confidentiality, be fully present, warmly supportive, and provide appropriate interventions if requested.

The experience of honestly sharing her life in front of another person and having her totally trust and accept her has a positive impact on her life. In Co-Counseling the experience is not just limited to one person. Starting in the Fundamentals training the new cocounselor has many different cocounseling partners thereby receiving the attention, concern, and acceptance of these separate and distinct people. No matter what a person works on or how she works on it, she sees the steady acceptance of each person with whom she is working. The new cocounselor begins to understand she is fully accepted within the community of cocounselors. She is not isolated in her problems and issues. She gradually comes to understand that, regardless of what she is working on, she is accepted and cared for by the people sitting across her.

This is not the conditional acceptance many of us experienced and continue to experience in our lives. Many people are raised in the world of conditional acceptance by well-intentioned parents who want their children to succeed in life. These parents focused on the shortcomings they wanted us to improve. They seldom praised the things we did well but instead stayed focused on how we could do things better. As children we internalize the attitudes of parents and other significant adults who wanted us to succeed and so continually pointed out our weaknesses. Sad to say, many of us today focus on our failings and give ourselves only conditional acceptance.

The self-acceptance we experience in Co-Counseling is not conditional—it is full, warm, and empowering. Starting in the Fundamentals training and continuing in gatherings and sessions, the positive energy of acceptance radiates through all our interactions. Session partners do not shy away from us after a session. People we cocounseled with in the past come up and hug us with a spirit of acceptance. The same hugs greet us at the door to gatherings. Warm, embracing hugs fill us with a deep sense of acceptance, especially compared to the societally accepted handshake with its clear implications of distance and separation.

As we do more and more sessions, we come to believe we are OK just the way we are. Meanwhile, we are gradually developing an intuitive sense about being human. No one is telling us we are human, but doing sessions with different people allows us to see that each of us struggles to live a good life. People's problems and issues may be different, but the *struggle with life* we all have in common. It crosses every dividing line separating us in the flimsy surface world of external comparisons—male-female, young-old, financially secure-insecure, and so on. Sitting in the co-counselor role, we see individuals struggle and we accept them as a fellow human struggling to live good lives. In this way we come to accept ourselves as good to the core and delightfully human.

Seeing ourselves as human helps us accept ourselves with all our blemishes and problems. We recognize our problems as uniquely ours, our history as uniquely ours, and our paths as uniquely ours. We are wonderful humans struggling to live the best life we can. Acknowledging ourselves as human gives us permission to accept ourselves as imperfect; moreover, it gives us not just the permission but the right and obligation to struggle as we move through the world.

The last step in reaching full self-acceptance is to forgive ourselves for all the negative judgments we have heaped on ourselves since childhood. Forgiving ourselves becomes a key part of the work we do as a self-counselor. We begin to appreciate how hard we have worked to get to exactly where we are now. There is no minimizing the effort and struggle we have endured. The self-appreciation we are now beginning to embrace opens the door to loving ourselves. *I appreciate and love myself with all my faults—* that is full self-acceptance. From this place we can begin to dance our dance and move our lives forward.

In an article about self-acceptance in *Psychology Today,* Leon Seltzer writes:

> To adopt a more loving stance toward ourselves—perhaps the *key* prerequisite for self-acceptance—we must develop a detachment that allows us to see ourselves as representative of *all* human beings . . . .[22]

This is what we do in Co-Counseling.

Chapter 41

The Power of Giving

Giving is the highest expression of potency. In the very act of giving, I experience my strength, my wealth, my power. This experience of heightened vitality and potency fills me with joy. I experience myself as overflowing, spending, alive, hence as joyous. Giving is more joyous than receiving not because it is a deprivation, but, because in the act of giving lies the expression of my aliveness.

—Erich Fromm, *The Art of Loving*

The basic responsibility of the co-counselor is to support the self-counselor. A person does this by *giving* caring-aware-attention, eye contact, touch, and whatever is requested in the session contract while holding confidentiality and maintaining the session space as safe. As a trainer I had said this hundreds of times; yet I had never thought of the act of *giving* as separate and distinct from what was being given. I focused only on what was being given—the caring-aware-attention, the touch, the eye contact, the interventions—and not the act of *giving* itself. The actuality of *giving* had very little meaning to me.

In *The Art of Loving* Erich Fromm examines the concept of giving. On the material level he says, "giving means being rich. Not he who has much is rich, but he who gives much." For the purpose of Co-Counseling, however, the significance of giving is on the human level, where we give of ourselves to another. And what is it we give? Fromm says we give "that which is alive in us."²³ And what is alive in us as we sit in the co-counselor role is our energy—our human energy. Our brain is *out with* the self-counselor. It is not thinking. We are *giving* caring-aware-attention to the self-counselor, and our brain is quiet.

As a trainer I don't tell people how to give caring-aware-attention. It is a concept that comes alive when they sit in the role of the co-counselor. No one has ever asked me, "How do I give caring-aware-attention?" Somehow this concept easily moves from an idea into a reality because it is about giving, and people know how to give of themselves to another person.

Near the end of the first night of the Fundamentals training, there is a six-minute exercise designed for people to get a glimpse of the power of giving caring-aware-at-tention. I invite everyone to pair up, and sit facing each other close enough to hold hands. I have them choose who will be the self-counselor first and then have the self-counselor set a contract by stating he wants caring-aware-attention and eye contact from the co-counselor, who consciously agrees to it. Then I tell the people in the self-counselor role what I want them to do during their six minutes: I invite them to close their eyes and meditate for the first two minutes; for the second two minutes I ask them to gaze at the co-counselor; and for the last two minutes I invite them to speak any thoughts that flow through their heads—*What you say doesn't have to make any sense,* I tell them—just talk without stopping. To the co-counselors I emphasize that their only re-sponsibility is to *give* caring-aware-attention and main-tain eye contact at all times. I also remind them not to judge or evaluate their self-counselors or what they are doing. Stay focused on *giving* caring-aware-attention, I repeat.

I then invite the self-counselors to close their eyes and meditate and start the timer. The room falls into silence. At each two-minute interval I remind the self-counselors what they are to do. At the end of the six minutes, the partners change roles. I restate what the self-counselors are to do in each two-minute segment and remind the people now in the co-counselor role that their main

275

responsibility is to *give* caring-aware-attention and eye contact.

I am always amazed at what happens in this exercise. When it is finished, there are two sharing rounds. In the first round people share how it was to be the co-counselor and to give caring-aware-attention. In the second round I ask them to share their experiences in the role of the self-counselor.

In the first sharing round almost all participants speak about feeling a sense of intimacy with the people sitting across from them with their eyes closed. They comment that, other than when looking at children or partners, they have never watched people with their eyes closed for that length of time—two long minutes. Almost all participants feel an instant liking for, and appreciation, of their partners. Many people say they felt protective of them. Some people talk about feeling their hearts beating in the silence. People express amazement at how many feelings passed through them as they simply gazed at their session partners during the two minutes.

During the second two minutes, when the self-counselor is gazing back at the co-counselor, a great deal of nervous energy floats through the room accompanied by giggles and, sometimes, laughter. People talk about how uncomfortable they felt during these two minutes.

New cocounselors are not used to looking directly into the eyes of another person who is gazing back at them. There is a shared intimacy in the eye gazing that experienced cocounselors become comfortable with, but it triggers nervousness in new people. The eye gaze breaks the normal boundaries of our personal space, resulting in an awkwardness bordering on embarrassment on the part of both session partners. The giggling during these two minutes represents the natural release of the embarrassment.

The third two minutes, in which the self-counselor is freely talking, is the most comfortable for the co-counselors because it closely resembles a social conversation. Some people comment on being unusually aware of the tone of voice, inflection, and hesitations in the voices of their self-counselors as well as how they were holding their bodies. Sometimes a person in the co-counselor role says he began feeling a liking for the self-counselor and felt a concern for the person as he was talking.

In general people feel good about themselves for giving the caring-aware-attention and eye contact that was expected of them. No one has ever said he had trouble giving the caring-aware-attention requested. People may have been nervous at first, but once settled into gazing at the face of the session partners in front of them, they relaxed. A sense of responsibility bubbles up in the

277

co-counselor, which speaks to the natural sense of caring people generate for each other when they feel safe.

In the second sharing round I invite people to talk about their experiences in the self-counselor role. During the first two minutes when their eyes were closed, people said they felt very safe. Many talk about feeling the co-counselor watching over them. Some experienced meditators comment on how easy it was for them to drop deeply into their meditation. During the mutual gazing segment, people felt the same discomfort and embarrassment as they did in the co-counselor role. Everyone expressed a sense of relief when the last two minutes arrived and they could finally talk. No one has ever said they had nothing to talk about. People feel cared for, and respected, by their co-counselors, who they have just met, and who simply sat in front of them giving caring-aware-attention and eye contact.

There is always a good dialogue on the relativity of time after the second round of sharing. The third segment always seems to go by the fastest and the mutual eye gaze goes slowest while the first segment is the most relative, with people having widely divergent senses of time both as the self-counselor and the co-counselor.

It general people feel good about what happened in the session. They are very energetic, and there is a buzz in the room despite it being about 10:00 p.m. when the exercise ends. So in the very first cocounseling session on the very first night of a Fundamentals training, people feel good about themselves because they were able to give the caring-aware-attention requested of them and felt the joy and power of giving it.

Chapter 42

Co-Counseling and the Capacity to Love

A problem shared is a problem halved.
Kindness in words creates confidence.
Kindness in thinking creates profoundness.
Kindness in giving creates love.

—Lao Tzu, Chinese philosopher

Love is the capacity to give without expectation of receiving anything in return. It is not dependent on a particular object outside us. Love is self-generating. It comes from within us and not from outside. Because of our cultural obsession with romantic love, we think of love only in terms of the pairing of romantic partners—Cupid, hearts, flowers, and kisses. Love is a natural instinct of the body to accept people for exactly who they are. Love involves feelings of caring for a person that transcends reason or logic. We naturally become attracted to, and have irrational sense of compatibility for, those we love. A strong sense of connection and identification arises naturally within us from the act of loving, while the warmth of our love energetically flows from us. We become attached to a person without the need to possess or own the individual. There is a vibrancy in loving that warms our hearts as we experience the loving. Love arises naturally when we feel free and safe; we cannot command it. Love is a natural passion existing within all of us.

Giving is the key to loving, and the giving in the co-counselor role unlocks the power of this wonderful, innate impulse. Giving caring-aware-attention proceeds from instinct rather than intellect. It is the attention a person gives when she feels open and is energetically connected to the person to whom she is giving the attention. This attention originates in the gut and heart rather than the brain. Giving is a disciplined, focused activity involving the energy a person naturally generates from within her body. It is always active and never passive.[24]

The co-counselor doesn't want or expect anything from the self-counselor. Her brain is silent. She is not involved in the content of her partner's work, and is, therefore, completely independent of that work. The co-counselor is not vested in the outcome of what the self-counselor is doing. Yet as the self-counselor openly reveals the most vulnerable and fragile aspects of her life, a natural rooting for her bubbles up from within the co-counselor's heart. The co-counselor starts seeing the whole person and, as she does, begins to experience the person as human. At this point the barriers separating the two people dissolve and a sense of intimacy springs forth with a genuine caring and concern for the self-counselor and her life.

With the external barriers gone, a true connection opens. The co-counselor feels a powerful, warm respect for the self-counselor along with a deepening sense of caring and concern, which evolves into a full-fledged sense of responsibility. The caring, respect, and responsibility are, according to Erich Fromm, the basic elements that demonstrate the active character of all forms of love.[25]

Being fully present in the co-counselor role as different people describe their problems and dilemmas, we begin to see each of them, not in their surface identity, but in their essential humanness struggling to live the best lives they can. The more people we share sessions with, the stronger the awareness becomes that we are all human and that all humans struggle. We don't need to know the specifics of what each self-counselor is working on to care for them as fellow humans striving to live a good, full, meaningful life. This type of generalized knowing is another key to loving. This knowing does not stay at the periphery or surface of our awareness, but penetrates deep to the very fabric of our being.

In our everyday world we separate ourselves from others based on their surface appearances or because of their ideas, attitudes, or beliefs. Once we pass through these differences to the humanness of a person the separation between us melts away, and as Fromm asserts, "I find myself, I discover myself, I discover us both, I discover man."[26] So in the process of giving caring-aware-attention and opening to the humanness of the self-counselor, the co-counselor discovers their humanity.

John Heron sees basic human helping, as practiced through the role of the co-counselor as, "The wise flow of love from person to person."[27] What turns on the tap of loving is seeing and experiencing the person in the self-counselor role as human. Once we transcend the individuality of a person whether in the self-counselor role or in other places in life, the tap turns on. We understand we are the same, and although circumstances have made us different, we can allow ourselves to act in a loving, caring manner. Thomas Merton, in *No Man is an Island,* states, "The beginning of love is to let those we love be perfectly themselves,"[28] which is exactly what the co-counselor does. There is no desire to change or control. There is the direct relationship of human to human.

The Co-counselor And The Art Of Giving

This is brotherly or sisterly love at its essence, and Co-Counseling, through the role of the co-counselor, allows people to experience this exciting connective feeling.

As our ability to see the humanness in a person grows, our ability to love her grows. In this human love we care for, respect, feel a sense of responsibility for, and possess a deep reverence for her honest struggling with life. We know her as an individual, and we know them as human.*

In Co-Counseling the people we work with do not stop being individuals, but more and more their wonderful humanness comes to the forefront of who we see and know. What attracts us is not the simple aura of being human but the reality of being human. Before our eyes, people shed the exterior appearances that keep us separate and emerge as humans we can relate to without judgment or bias. As we see the human in everyone our world changes—our perception of reality changes. We now see a person's humanity, and that perspective allows us to relate with, understand, and see them shining and as good to the core.

People in the co-counselor role are not busy "loving" the self-counselors with whom they do sessions. They are giving them caring-aware-attention not love. Love is never mentioned in cocounseling trainings—it cannot be taught. People build the capacity to love within the sacredness of sessions and this love, anchored in our common humanity, radiates into the community of co-counselors. The ability to feel and express love may occur in Co-Counseling more easily than in ordinary life because we learned not to be afraid of our emotions and the energy of emotions is similar to the energy of love and as we continue to practice Co-Counseling our ability to feel and express love becomes easier. (Note: This can become a problem. A person can find himself or herself *falling in love* with their cocounseling partner. This type of romantic and sexual attraction is discussed in the Fundamentals training and suggestions are presented if such an attraction begins.)

This ability to love with the elements of trust, respect, responsibility, and the knowledge that we are all wonderfully human, breaks down the barriers that keep most people apart. In small support groups, in gatherings, and at large international conferences, people come together in joy and anticipate a good time doing sessions; they share new ideas about what we can be done in sessions, and broaden the scope, understanding, and use of Co-Counseling in the modern world. John Heron has said, and I firmly believe, that Co-Counseling as an organization needs to inquire constantly into itself in the same way individuals who cocounsel inquiry into themselves. Within the spaciousness of an international gathering generous amount of human love and respect flow through the participants as they work and play in the spirit of human acceptance and equality.

Chapter 44

Self-love and Final Thoughts

Love arouses soulness
Brings warmth and strength
to
everyone
. . .
Melts away loneliness

Co-Counseling has a particular beauty in that it can serve many people in exactly the way they need to be served. Co-Counseling involves many things and does not posit a single path or goal for the work done using it.

Co-Counseling is a practice and process in which we learn
- a set of skills to explore our lives and to change our lives *as we choose*
- to be self-directed and honest about our lives

- to make friends with our emotions
- to know ourselves and others as human

Co-Counseling has a set of beliefs about being human
- We are all good to the core.
- We have all our answers inside ourselves.

Co-Counseling has a distinct culture in which people
- embrace each other as good to the core
- honor sacred space and the use of ritual
- hold confidentiality in sessions and sharing circles

Within the safety of Co-Counseling we learn
- to be truthful with ourselves about ourselves
- to meditate on the humanness of others
- to appreciate the power of setting personal contracts
- to reach inside and give fully of ourselves

Co-Counseling is learning to accept ourselves and
- to appreciate ourselves
- to see ourselves as human
- to have a sacred relationship with ourselves
- to see ourselves as perfectly imperfect

- to experience and know the depth and power of love

Co-Counseling teaches us the value of
- taking refuge in sessions, support groups, gatherings, and community
- making conscious decisions
- trusting and loving ourselves

Co-Counseling does not mandate goals for practitioners; however, the longer people maintain their practice, the more they set directions and goals for themselves. Cocounselors can use their practice to pursue these directions and goals. Self-counselors are self-directed and so the choice is always theirs to choose what they do and how they do it. Co-Counseling gives people the freedom to be who they are and pursue whatever they choose to pursue.

Co-counseling is a practice and not a perfect. There is no nirvana or heaven to be reached. Niek Sickenga, a Dutch Co-Counselor, likes to say Co-Counseling is about making peace with the past, the present, and the future. I like his idea and would rephrase it simply to say: Co-Counseling is about making peace with ourselves. There is a lot of work involved in reaching a place of internal peace.

THE CO-COUNSELOR AND THE ART OF GIVING

Inner peace seems like a worthwhile goal for all humans. But before we can make peace with ourselves we need to see and acknowledge ourselves as human. From the vantage point of our humanness, we can accept the need to struggle. Why do we struggle? We struggle because we have the gift of consciousness and awareness. We make hundreds of decisions every day. Many are not easy, even if the choices are clear. And so we struggle. We can curse the struggle, resist making the decision, or bury our heads and let fate make the choice for us. As humans we struggle, and accepting the struggle makes our life easier.

From the vantage point of our own humanity, we can develop the self-compassion and self-understanding that leads to self-acceptance. We cannot hate part of ourselves or hold shame about something buried in the past if we are to fully embrace ourselves. Moving closer and closer to full self-acceptance we begin the process of forgiveness, especially self-forgiveness. We cannot fully accept ourselves if we are judging ourselves to be bad and wrong for what we have done in the past or are doing in the present. Nor can we accept ourselves if we are busy blaming others for our shortcomings and problems. Self-acceptance requires full self-responsibility, and that self-responsibility has to be gentle and loving.

On the way to making peace with ourselves, we develop compassion for others and ourselves. As we come to know ourselves we learn to be gentle with ourselves, and as we learn to be gentle with ourselves we learn to be gentle with others. We foster self-acceptance and grow a love and appreciation for ourselves with all our blemishes, wounds, joys, and passions. At the same time we learn to accept others in the same way. This is the place of inner peace, and surrounding and guarding this space within us is self-love. When I speak of *self-love* I am not talking about the egotistical, narcissistic, pompous shell people wear to cover their insecurities. I am talking about a self-love that loves and accepts the world and being in the world. I am talking about being grateful for every aspect and event in our lives. This love is what protects our inner peace. This is true self-love.

Brené Brown considers self-love and self-acceptance "almost revolutionary." She sees "Loving and accepting ourselves "as the ultimate acts of courage" in our society.[29] Yet they seem to flow naturally out of the practice of Co-Counseling. Inner peace is the magical home we need to reach in order to bring real change into our lives. From this place of calmness and certitude, we can see clearly the journey we are on from birth to death. In this place intuition and inspiration flow and the choices we make feel certain even without having an explanation.

We need to love ourselves in order to bring about the changes necessary to create a life we love. There is no rational, logical sequence of thought that can conceive of the new ideas necessary to create this life. A concept attributed to Albert Einstein speaks to this very notion. New ideas can happen only through an *intuitive leap* based on an *intellectual love of the objects of experience*. The self-love we acquire cocounseling comes from our head, our heart, and our gut. It matches the *intellectual love* of Einstein and allows us to use our intuition to create to new ideas about ourselves that leap beyond the self-limiting images we acquired in childhood. Within the timeless, sacred space of session work we can find, not only new possibilities for our lives but create the plans to bring those possibilities into reality. In these sessions our self-appreciation, love, and inner peace give birth to the self we have always wanted to be.

It is not easy to live continuously from the place of inner peace. Our world bombards us with difficult choices and hostile voices. Our self-love can and does desert us, and when it does, our inner peace can flounder. But once we know we can love ourselves, we can find the source of the dis-ease that caused us to lose the self-love. Co-Counseling sessions, with their peacefulness, self-direction, and human support, are the perfect place to discover and rediscover our self-love and the serenity of inner peace.

Maintaining
Our Practice

Support Groups

Unity of spirit
The earth . . . universe . . . all of us
What a grand mixing bowl!

John Heron has posited three basic human needs: to be
loved, to be understood, and to be self-directed.[30] These
needs are not easily met and appreciated in our world.
Even when we are children, these needs—our needs—
can be frustrated. A child has the need to be loved; yet
parents, despite all of their love for the child, make their
love conditional on the child's staying on the path the
parents believe will best serve him. The need to be understood can be difficult to satisfy when children have
yet to acquire the ability to articulate what it is they want
and why they want it. And lastly, everyone knows who is in
charge, and it is not the child.

Here I look at these three needs, not as they impact the
child but as they impact the adult. To be self-directed,

understood, and loved is not common within our modern world. Many people do not feel understood and loved in an open and satisfying way. The issue of being self-directed is a constant challenge as the demands of jobs and family weigh a person down. For those who are unemployed, the issue of being self-directed may even be greater because they feel at the whim of society.

I periodically meet with a group of men, most of whom have taken the Fundamentals training. They ground me in the persistent issues facing middle-class, middle-aged men living in twenty-first-century America, especially after the economic collapse of 2008. They have struggled financially, having been bumped from jobs and lost businesses. Relationships have been strained and changed. They have been thrown back on their own resources and have shown tremendous resilience in the face of new and difficult obstacles. They are survivors. I feel honored to be invited into their circle.

These men meet every other week alternating among the homes of its members. They share a meal when they arrive, during which they exchange details about recent happenings in their lives along with comments on the food. After clearing the table, we gather in another room, form a circle, join hands, close our eyes, and ground ourselves in our bodies by focusing on our breath—consciously breathing in and making a noise on the exhale.

We do this several times, and the sounds get louder and more powerful each time. Vocalizing on the exhale allows each of us to let out some of the stored energy we carry within us while awakening our inner voice, which lays dormant until it knows it is safe to come forward. We then open our eyes; look around appreciating each other, and share validations and something new and good in our lives. Many people find validating themselves and finding new and good things in their lives to be hard, but not this group of men. No matter what is happening in their lives, they find the inner strength to celebrate themselves and the positive aspects of their lives.

This opening circle marks the ritual beginning of the gathering and separates the socializing of the evening meal from the sacred space we share as a men's group. In this space we honor confidentiality and silently give caring-aware-attention to whoever is sharing. With the ritual opening complete, we settle into the evening with a "check-in," sharing briefly what is going on in our exterior and interior lives. The trust level in this group is amazing. Imbued with this trust, each man's vivid description of his daily struggles touches everyone else present. The gut power of the sharing seems to put all of us into an alert stillness; every nuance in the voice of the person sharing is heard and respected. (Several men are part of 12-step meetings, and their sharing often touches upon the details of their experience in these.)

After the check-in we break up into dyads and do an hour session, which allows each man thirty minutes in the role of the self-counselor. At one meeting a new man was present whom I had briefed on the basic form of Co-Counseling during dinner. When we broke into dyads, I paired up with him. Rather than each of us doing one thirty-minute period as the self-counselor, we did four fifteen-minute periods, alternating times in the two roles. In Co-Counseling we hold confidentiality seriously, so I cannot comment on the work this man did. What I can say is the basics of Co-Counseling are so natural that even a person who has no experience can give caring-aware-attention and share from the heart when he is given the space and the free attention of an experienced cocounselor. What he did share with me afterward is that, although he is not a talker, he probably shared more in his two fifteen-minutes periods as the self-counselor than he has maybe ever shared and that he felt comfortable doing so.

A regular member of the group is also not a talker. He says he hates to come to the group because he knows he will talk. At the end of the evening, however, he always says he feels lighter and more hopeful. The only thing he has done is speak the truth of his life in front of a person who did not judge him or try to "fix" him. The struggles and problems he is experiencing in his life have been witnessed and, in the witnessing, have been validated. This is incredibly simple, but to speak our gut truth uninterrupted and without fear of judgment is rare in our world, and doing it feels good.

When sessions are complete, we come back together and do a sharing round. Some men talk about how they feel after the session compared to how they felt earlier in the evening. Others share the content of their work. They do this to acknowledge in front of the whole group a truth they have discovered or an action plan they will be following. By speaking the truth or describing the plan out loud, they also reinforce it within themselves, helping them bring it into their ongoing lives.

Then, joining hands, we do a closing circle with rounds of validations, gratitudes, and something we are taking from the evening. In this way we ritualize the ending our meeting. What follows are hugs, appreciations, and the business of the next meeting. The men hop into their cars and drive away leaving the man whose house we met in with lots of positive energy, and the final cleanup from the dinner.

In this group the three basic human needs are met, bringing forth an openness and honesty that sustain the deeply personal connection these men share with each other. Their understanding of each other moves beyond a general acceptance of the needs and issues of being human; these men know each other as men with the problems and issues that face men struggling to maintain a foothold in an unstable economic world. Living in the same geographic area, and experiencing the economic and social world in similar ways, their understanding of each other is real and empathetic. They leave these meetings having been heard and understood, which is part of what holds the group together.

The human need to love and be loved shows up as each man walks in the door. He is greeted with hugs and humor. Everyone stops what he is doing and gives his attention to the man. The spirit of acceptance and love flows in these greetings. Love implies respect, knowledge, caring, and responsibility, and these men extend these qualities to each other. The caring and respect is obvious all evening. The responsibility begins with the commitment to show up; close down their smart phones; and be present for, honest with, and aware of each other. These men share a knowledge of each other that is probably greater than how anyone else knows them. To love another is to be concerned with his growth and happiness. This element of love rings absolutely true with these men.

Something transformative happens to each man, including me when I am in this group. The brotherly love present here is palpable, and being immersed in it allows each man to feel a deep self-appreciation. By being there, each man is affirming his belief in his own life and his desire for growth and happiness, which is what love is about. Without love of the self there can be no genuine love of others. The first of the golden rules of Christianity is to "love thy neighbor as thyself." Without truly loving the self, which is an "affirmation of one's own life, happiness, growth, [and] freedom . . ." there cannot be real love of others.[31] The two go hand in hand.

Lastly, the human need to be self-directed means having the ability to make meaningful choices that lead to action. In this group men make conscious decisions about their lives and act on them. That is what they do. That is one of the main reasons they meet. All the men in the group make the decision to attend the group and, while there, are totally free to do what they want or need to do.

One less obvious quality of the Co-Counseling culture and practice is this very human desire to be understood, loved, and self-directed. There are simply not many places in our world where these three human needs are so abundantly met. They are present when two people meet to do a session and in the support groups that grow out of the Co-Counseling trainings and gatherings. These groups may be structured like the men's group I attend, or they may choose to do most of their work in the group as a whole.

Each support group sets up its own structure and procedures. Support groups form around identifiable characteristics such as men's groups and women's groups, or they may be a generic group that has a geographic base. In Michigan they have a system of directing people into support groups while they are taking an extended fundamentals training. At all large national and international workshops, small support groups are formed and provide people the opportunity to work intimately with a small number of people. Besides bringing intimacy to large gatherings, these support groups provide individuals the time and space to process what is happening for them within the larger workshops.

Wherever and however support groups are formed, and whatever their structure, they become a refuge for their members. These groups allow each person to see and relate to each other as human with all the greatness and failings of being human. The more the group meets, the more the members grow to truly understand and have empathy for each other's struggles and joys. Support groups are safe havens for members to be completely truthful about what is happening in their lives. Here they are self-directed, loved, and understood. What better place is therein our modern world?

Whether we are talking about sessions, support groups, gatherings, or large national or international conferences, cocounselors bathe in the loving positive energy that flows from the Co-Counseling well and emerge refreshed mentally, emotionally, and spiritually. Our spirits soar as we wash the dross of daily living from our psychic and emotional beings. This binds cocounselors together. The respect, knowledge, caring, and sense of responsibility moving through sessions and gatherings bring forth a sense of gratitude in those present while grounding them in their own humanness. Love is not taught in Co-Counseling but flows abundantly wherever cocounselors meet.

Appendix A:

Vision of Co-Counseling International

a personal account of the core of CCI by John Heron
(one of the founders of Co-Counseling International)
October 2009, revised 13 December 2010

This is my vision of what CCI has the potential to be, and is, in my view, in the process of becoming:

1. I see CCI as a worldwide federation of independent local self-help communities whose members are trained to become competent in whole person development.

2. This development includes at least seven dynamically interrelated paths:

- Opening to the spiritual and the subtle, especially the presence between autonomous and cooperative peers.

- Celebration and validation of self and others and the wider world.

- Nurturance and self-care.

- Healing past and present emotional trauma by catharsis, transmutation and re-evaluation.

- Artistic expression of unfolding insights.

- Creative thinking, problem-solving, and the life-enhancing transformation of personal beliefs.

- Goal-setting and action-planning for personal, social and planetary flourishing.

3. Members are trained to work in pairs, taking turns to be in the primary role of self-directed worker [self-counselor] and in the supportive role of co-worker [co counselor].

The worker always keeps some attention outside their work within any path in order creatively to direct that work, and also to be alert to switch to any other path that calls to make its contribution.

Before starting work, the worker chooses the contract in terms of which any facilitation is offered by the co-worker, whose basic support within every contract is to give unrestricted free attention to the worker's emergence.

4. The CCI belief system affirms that the guiding authority for the work of personal development manifests in a uniquely creative way within each worker, an idiosyncratic personal authority which is refined in the crucible of validation and facilitation by co-workers.

5. Within the CCI worldwide federation there is no central control of anything.

Local communities are self-organizing with regard to the training and accreditation of teachers, and to the schedule of basic and advanced workshops and other developmental events.

International workshops held regularly in various parts of Europe, the USA and New Zealand [and Israel], provide a forum for sharing differences of local approaches, for co-creative hybridization between them, and also for stimulating ongoing international discussions online.

This kind of mutual education and collaborative inquiry makes possible a forward movement of basic CCI beliefs and practices, the soundness and validity of which are thereby enhanced by a continuous, ongoing and informal kind of participatory action research.

6. Leadership within CCI communities is a spontaneous, emergent phenomenon, where different members at different times, validated and supported by their peers to do so, take initiatives to train newcomers, and to organize and facilitate a wide range of peer support, development and inquiry groups for established members. This kind of leadership of an event is primarily authenticated by the degree to which it enhances the personal autonomy and interpersonal co-operation and co-creativity of those participating in it.

7. There is no one exclusively valid account of the core of CCI. Validity is a social phenomenon, progressively built up by the way in which a whole range of individual accounts both overlap to empower each other, and also have differences of style, emphasis and content to enrich and complement each other with idiosyncratic personal wisdom.

8. The CC in the acronym CCI can stand for different titles: "Co-counselling" to bring out CCI's historical roots, "Co-creation" to affirm its innovative developmental work, "Co-operative Culture" to assert its status as a leading form of peer to peer social organization.

Appendix B:

International Contact People

Australia

Skye FitzPatrick
Freshwater, NSW, Australia
suzenmea@yahoo.com.au

Belgium

Marie McNicholas
Brussels, Belgium
mc@collectifs.net

Canada

Wafik Raouf
Newmarket, Ontario,
Canada
wafik_raouf@yahoo.com

Germany

Markus Papenberg
Münster, Germany
markus.papenberg@web.de

Hungary

Saci László
Budapest, Hungary
saci.laszlo@gmail.com

Iceland

Lowana Veal
Reykjavik, Iceland
lowana@peace.is

Ireland

Declan Reddy
Dublin, Ireland
reddy.jd88@gmail.com

Israel

Janice Wasser
Tel Aviv, Israel
janice.wasser@gmail.com

Netherlands

www.cocounseling.nl

New Zealand / Aotearoa

Virginia deJoux
Wellington, New Zealand
virginia.dejoux@xtra.co.nz

Scotland

Rose Evision
Pitlochry, Scotland
changestrategies@
changeweaver.co.uk

Sri Lanka

Sushila Raja
Colombo, Sri Lanka
sushila.raja@gmail.com

United Kingdom

Sue Gray
Woodbridge, England
contactsue@yahoo.co.uk

United States

Fred Wallace
New Haven, CT
earthfred90@gmail.com

Within United States

East Coast – Fred Wallace
Midwest – Gaia Kile
a2cocounseling@gmail.com
West Coast – Yvonne Burgess
Ymburgess@gmail.com

Appendix C:

Websites about Co-Counseling International

CCI World News Service http://cciwns.com (in English)

By Dutch cocounselor - news and great archives

New Zealand   http://www.coco.org.nz

Israel   http://dror.org.il/en/home
                       (in English)

Dror community website, info on Dror way of cocounselling

Netherlands (in Dutch) http://www.co-counseling.nl

Germany (in German)   http://www.haus-kloppenburg.
                       de

Info about CCI in Münster at Haus Kloppenburg

Germany (in German)   http://www.co-counseln-lernen.
                       de

By Rudolph Giesselman about learning cocounseling

Ireland   http://www.catalase.com/coco.htm

United Kingdom   http://co-counselling.info

Info about CCI cocounseling in UK, part public, part members

United Kingdom   http://co-counselling.co.uk

By Richard Mills) info on co-counselling and courses in Leeds

United Kingdom   http://www.cocolh.co.uk

Site specific for summer gathering at Laurieston Hall

Scotland   http://www.cocoscotland.co.uk

Scotland   http://co-counselling.info/en/wiki/

United States   http://www.cci-usa.org

United States   http://www.cocowell.life

John Heron   http://www.human-inquiry.com
(check CoCo papers)

Endnotes

1   John Heron, "Co-Counselling Manual," (Podere Gello, San Cipriano, Volterra, Italy, revised1998), 5.

2   Margaret Christie, *The Oboist's Bedside Book.* (Glenrothes, Fife, England: HappenStance Press, 2007)

3   Carlos Castaneda, *The Teachings of Don Juan a Yaqui Way of Knowledge* and subsequent books, (New York: Ballantine Books, 1969)

4   Leonard Orr, and Sondra Ray, *Rebirthing in the New Age*, (Berkeley, CA: Celestial Arts, December 1977.)

5   Paul Ekman Ph.D. *Emotions Revealed* (New York: Owl Books, 2007)

6   Charles Duhigg, *The Power of HABIT*, p. Xvi.(New York: Random House, 2012), xvi.

7   Daniel Goleman and Tara Bennett-Goleman, "RELIEVING STRESS: MIND OVER MUSCLE," The New York Times, September 28, 1986

8   Hawkins, David, *Power vs. Force*, (Carlsbad, CA: Hay House, Inc., 2002)

9   James A. Garfield, The Quote Garden, http://www.
    quotegarden.com/truth.html

10 Herman Melville, *Moby Dick,* (New York: Signet Classics,
    2013), 1.

11 Carl Rogers, *On Becoming a Person,* (Boston: Houghton
    Miffin Company, 1961), 33.

12 Kurt Kuenne, "Validation", www.youtube.com/
    watch?v=Cbk980jV7Ao

13 Mitch Albom, *Tuesdays with Morey,* (New York: Doubleday
    Books, 1997), 35.

14 Heron, *Helping the Client,* 243.

15 Robert Hunter and Jerry Garcia, (1986). Touch of Grey
    [Recorded by the Grateful Dead] on *In the Dark* [LP].
    New York, NY: Arista Records. (1987)

16 Brené Brown, *The Gift of Imperfection,* (Center City:
    Minnesota, 2010), 39.

17 Andrew Hunt and David Thomas *The Pragmatic
    Programmer: From Journeyman to Master.* (Reading,
    Massachuettes: Addison-Wesley, Longman, 1999), 95,
    footnote

18 http://c2.com/cgi/wiki?ThinkingOutLoud

19 Fred Wallace, "The New Parent Count," unpublished poem

20 Rose Evison and Richard Horobin, "Co-Counselling as
    Therapy" (Sheffield, England: CO- COUNSELLING
    PHOENIX, 1994), 10.

ENDNOTES

[21] Thich Nhat Hanh, *Miracle of Mindfulness, A Manual on Meditation*, (Boston: Beacon Press, 1997), 7.

[22] Leon F. Seltzer, Ph.D, http://www.psychologytoday.com/blog/evolution-the-self/200809/the-path-unconditional-self-acceptance

[23] Erich Fromm, *The Art of Loving*, (New York: Bantam Books, 1972), 20.

[24] Heart Math Institute, (HeartMath.com)

[25] Fromm, *The Art of Loving*, 22.

[26] Ibid., 26.

[27] Heron, *Helping the Client*, 11.

[28] Thomas Merton, *No Man Is an Island*, (www.brainyquote.com/quotes/quotes/t/thomasmert121801.html)

[29] Brown, *The Gift of Imperfection*, 30.

[30] Heron, *Helping the Client*, 244

[31] Fromm p. 50

About the Author

Fred Wallace was born in New Haven, Connecticut. Holding numerous degrees from the University of Connecticut, he launched a career working in drug rehab centers, consulting for small towns and nonprofit organizations, and serving as the executive director of several public housing authorities.

Having practiced Vipassana meditation, tai chi, and yoga for many years, he eventually became a certified instructor of rebirthing and transformational breathing. A cocounseling teacher since 1990, Wallace has also served as part of the organizational leadership of Co-Counseling International–USA, was a charter member of Co-Counseling International Teachers of Northeastern United States, and has served on the organizing committee of the Connecticut Men's Gathering. He is a member of a co-creating inquiry group that meets throughout the year. He has instructed hundreds of students in New England, California, New Zealand, and Europe, and led many personal growth workshops.

Wallace lives in his hometown. He has one daughter and one grandson.

For more information visit: www.cocowell.life

www.ingramcontent.com/pod-product-compliance
Lightning Source LLC
LaVergne TN
LVHW011216080426
835509LV00005B/163